ADHD - RAISING AN EXPLOSIVE CHILD

A MIND-BODY PARENTING APPROACH TO THRIVE
FROM DISTRACTION HYPERACTIVE CHILDHOOD.
HOW TO UNDERSTAND ADD AND LEARN NEW
EMOTIONAL CONTROL STRATEGIES TO SELF-
REGULATE IN ADULTHOOD

D1637287

THERESA MILLER

Congratulation on purchasing this Book and thank you for doing so.

Please enjoy!

About The Author

~

THERESA MILLER is a cognitive therapist focusing on the treatment of anxiety and addiction, committed to studying and researching methods to complement therapy - a line of work she continues to pursue successfully among her patients.

She is particularly interested of affective vulnerability factors, such as distress intolerance and attachment, that are common across psychological disorders, with a focus on those that can be modified with behavioral treatment.

Her research is also focused on the behavioral therapies: although these are already highly effective for a number of psychiatric disorders, there is room for improvements.

Her first work as an author, published over one year ago, had been "Best Seller" in the Anxiety Disorder books category for a long time, but it is advisable to get also the audiobook version of it.
(free the first month, on Audible).

Her passion is to help adults and teenager, supporting them to achieve a better quality of life by confronting issues of depression, anxiety, stress, and low self-esteem, and showing them how to use the mind to detox from toxic behaviors.

THERESA MILLER is an impact maker who aspires to bring out the best in everyone she comes in contact with.

~

Follow her for more and new updates on fb →

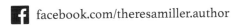 facebook.com/theresamiller.author

COPYRIGHT

CONTENTS

INTRODUCTION

Approximately 11 percent of all children in the United States are diagnosed with attention deficit hyperactivity disorder (ADHD). It is a neurodevelopmental disorder that can interfere with a child's academic and personal life.

The statistics for children who suffer from ADHD are profound. The symptoms first appear between the ages of three and six, while the average age of children who are diagnosed is seven. Approximately 6 percent of children in the United States are treated for ADHD with stimulant or nonstimulant medication.

Most staggering of all is the fact that there has been a 42 percent increase in the number of children diagnosed with ADHD in the past eight years.

This book is designed to help you through the challenges that ADHD creates. An introduction to ADHD can help you understand the disability and symptoms. You will learn about getting a diagnosis and what that entails.

Perhaps most importantly, you will learn about different treatments available and what you can do to help your child become a successful adult while keeping yourself healthy.

It is important to note that although boys and men are three times more likely to be diagnosed with ADHD, girls and women do still often suffer from the disability too. If your child is diagnosed with ADHD, please remember that you are not alone in your journey!

CHAPTER ONE: WHAT IS ADHD, WHAT ARE THE SYMPTOMS, AND WHEN SHOULD I GET MY CHILD EVALUATED?

*Y*ou are losing your mind when your son's first grade teacher, Mrs. Paris, calls for the second time in a week. It seems that your son, little Charlie, is having a few issues in class. Today, she reports that when he came in from recess, he refused to sit down and work on his math assignment. Instead, he picked up his chair, acted like he was attached to it, and raced around the room. She suggests that perhaps it might be time to have Charlie evaluated for ADHD.

At first, you are resistant. Everyone has heard the squirrel jokes associated with ADHD. You know, the one that goes, "I was talking to my friend, oh look a squirrel." And Charlie can focus on activities when he wants to. After all, he can play his games for hours without moving. However, ADHD is more complicated than that. There are many symptoms associated with ADHD, and the correct diagnosis and treatment can mean a life changing difference for you and your child.

What Is ADHD?

Attention deficit hyperactivity disorder is more than a simple inability to sit still or stay focused on a task for very long. It is a neurodevelopmental disorder that affects social, academic, and other functions. Like other neurodevelopmental disorders, ADHD manifests itself early in your child's development, usually before they start school. It is not diagnosed until specific symptoms are exhibited. Most kids are diagnosed when they are around seven years old. Sometimes, a child may be diagnosed when they are older, but it is very likely that they had some of the symptoms when they were younger.

How do you know if your precious baby has ADHD or is just acting like a normal kid their age? There are specific signs that may point to the answer.

Each person may show different signs of ADHD. Just like so many other mental and physical health issues, ADHD is not a one-size-fits-all disorder, making it difficult to diagnose ADHD.

Signs and Symptoms

One sign of ADHD is if your child shows self-focused behavior. they are unable to perceive other people's needs and desires. They might interrupt conversations or activities and may be unable to wait their turn, either in games or classroom activities. Likewise, they could also frequently interrupt people when they are talking or inserting themselves into conversations, games, etc., that they are not a part of.

Another sign of ADHD is if your child is unable to control their emotions, especially anger. These emotions may be displayed at inappropriate times. Younger children might display this trait through temper tantrums.

Constant movement and fidgeting are also symptoms of ADHD. They might be unable to sit down for long periods. If they are forced to sit, they might fidget or wiggle around a lot. In addition, they might be unable to play quietly for very long.

Another struggle that they might face is in completing tasks. They might start on their homework, then notice that a few things in their room are out of place. They start to clean their room but notice their Lego project has a few pieces missing. They then begin to work on that, then—you get the idea. They might find it difficult to stay engaged, even with projects and tasks they are really interested in.

To go along with the inability to finish tasks is a difficulty to focus on anything. They may struggle to pay attention in class or even to a conversation that they are actively engaged in. You might be talking to him about the latest game that all the kids are playing. Partway through the conversation, their mind wanders off to the last time they played the game and how the other person must have cheated to beat them, etc.

"Are you listening to me?" you ask. They nod but can't tell you what you said.

Tasks that take a lot of mental effort are also difficult for kids with ADHD, thus they tend to avoid them whenever possible. This can include homework, paying attention to instructions, or even reading.

Planning may also be a weakness for kids who struggle with ADHD. It isn't because they are lazy or not intelligent enough to follow through with the instructions or steps necessary. It is simply because they struggle with following instructions, especially if they have several steps or aspects to them. This can lead to them making careless mistakes.

Although the inability to sit still for long periods is a hallmark of ADHD, your kid might also simply be withdrawn. They might ignore what is happening around them and refuse to become involved with class activities or even play time activities with their peers. They may simply stare off into space, daydream, and completely ignore what is going on around them.

Organization is an issue for a lot of people. It is even more of an issue for kids who suffer from ADHD. They have problems keeping track of their tasks and other activities. They might also struggle with prioritizing their tasks and activities, including their homework.

"Mom, do you know where I put my _____?" Is this a common question in your house? This could be the case because kids with ADHD tend to be more forgetful than their peers. They might forget to do their homework, chores, or other tasks. They may often misplace their toys and other belongings.

Some of symptoms might change or escalate as they get older. A lot of these symptoms can make your child seem less mature than their peers. One problem they might have as they get older is understanding social cues from other people.

The focus on homework and other tasks is still an issue. They might struggle with compromising with others, helping with chores and other tasks at home, and managing their time wisely. In addition, their hygiene may become an issue. Another problem might arise when he gets his driver's license, because sometimes, people who have ADHD do not drive as safely as other people.

As stated, not all kids will struggle with all these symptoms; likewise, they could struggle with different issues to various degrees. However, if your child shows at least a couple symptoms at home and school regularly, you might consider getting them evaluated for ADHD. This is especially true if the symptoms interfere with their success at school or prevent them from developing and maintaining positive relationships with peers, family, and other people.

What Is the Difference Between ADHD and ADD?

Attention deficit disorder, or ADD, has symptoms that include the inability to focus, concentrate, or pay attention, being easily distracted, and having a bad working memory. If your child spends a lot of time daydreaming and is uninterested and disorganized, then their diagnosis might be more in line with ADD. Although the term is still used, ADD is no longer an official diagnosis. Rather, the diagnosis is a type of ADHD and is called *predominantly inattentive type*.

A diagnosis of ADHD has the additional symptoms of hyperactivity and impulsiveness. They might be fidgety and full of energy. They could have trouble waiting their turn and tend to have behavior problems.

Primarily Inattentive Type

There are several symptoms of primarily inattentive type of ADHD. Your child might have this type of ADHD if they are forgetful, have trouble focusing, and have poor organizational and listening skills. This type of ADHD may be mistaken for a mood disorder, since your child might seem apathetic to what is happening around them. Your child might not pay attention to details and make careless mistakes. They might also be unable to pay attention in class, to homework, or other tasks for very long. It often seems like they aren't paying attention when people talk to them. They don't follow instructions and will often not finish projects they have started. They will lose items that are necessary to complete tasks or activities. He dislikes any task or activity that requires a sustained mental effort, and will often avoid them if he can.

Hyperactive Impulsive ADHD

This type of ADHD is often depicted by a child swinging off the chandelier and literally bouncing off the walls. However, not everyone who suffers from this type of ADHD exhibits that type of hyperactivity.

Many children who suffer from hyperactive impulsive ADHD do have trouble sitting still for long periods. They might not run around in circles all day, but they might be restless and fidget a lot. The DSM-V states that your child must show six of the nine main symptoms in order to be diagnosed with this type of ADHD.

One symptom that your child might show if they have this type of ADHD is that they fidget with their hands or feet a lot or squirm around in their chair. They might also have trouble staying in their chair in class or other times. They might run around and climb on things a little too often when they are expected to be still.

Older children might feel restless a lot of the time. He might not be able to play quietly. They may resemble the Energizer Bunny Rabbit in that they keep on going and going and going, as though they have a motor inside of them. They might also talk a lot and blurt out answers in class instead of waiting to be called on. They might have problems waiting for their turn in games or other activities. They could also interrupt other people or intrude on conversations that other people are having.

Combined Type ADHD—Inattentive ADHD

Some children actually suffer from primarily inattentive type ADHD *and* hyperactive impulsive ADHD. They would be diagnosed with this type if they have at least six symptoms from both types.

One symptom of inattentive ADHD is making careless mistakes. An example of this is if your child rushes through their test and gets some answers wrong, even if they know the answers. They might even skip entire sections of the test simply because they weren't paying attention.

They might be unable to pay attention to games, activities, or other organized tasks for very long. They could be unable to read for long periods or pay attention to long conversations.

Another symptom is not listening, even when someone is talking directly to them. They might seem as though they are absent-minded when someone is talking, even if there are no obvious distractions around them. They might not finish their homework, chores, or other tasks, and may not follow through when given instructions. They may start the activities but will be unable to focus for very long.

Being unable to stay organized is another symptom of this type of ADHD. Their locker is a mess, their room is a mess, and they can never find their school work. This leads to an inability to manage time well and finding it difficult to meet deadlines.

Long homework assignments or other activities that require a lot of steps may be a particular challenge for your child. Because these tasks seem so overwhelming, your child will simply avoid them altogether, even if it means getting a bad grade in class.

Does your child constantly lose things? Is their key phrase "Mom, where is my_____?" Losing things often, such as their phone, glasses, homework, toys, etc., is another symptom of combined type ADHD.

"I wanted to complete the _____... oh look, a squirrel," is the catch-phrase for this type of ADHD. Children may be easily distracted by anything extra going on around them. They might also just simply daydream, drift off into their own world, and lose focus on the task at hand.

Forgetfulness is another symptom of this type of ADHD. They might forget to turn in work or complete their chores.

Diagnosing ADHD

You get phone calls from school about your child's behavior. At home, he never stops squirming, throws food at his brother, and has explosive anger. He can't focus on his homework and instead blows spitballs at his sister, laughing at the several tiny white pieces of paper that decorate her hair. By the end of the night, his sister is ready to beat him up, his little brother is biting his ankles, and you are ready to go on a long vacation.

Is it ADHD? Perhaps. The only way to know is to talk to a doctor for an official diagnosis. There is no specific test for ADHD. Usually, when you take your child to the doctor, the doctor can take their temperature and some blood, listen to symptoms, and then you can deduce what the problem is.

In this case, not all doctors are created equal, and that includes their knowledge of ADHD and their ability to diagnose it accurately. That leads to the question of figuring out whether your child suffers from ADHD or if there are other issues. There do exist some steps that you can take.

The first step is when you begin to think that your child's issues might stem from something beyond just being a kid. Their teacher calls you more than your family members because they are constantly disrupting class and are falling behind in all of their lessons. Your boss tells you that if you are late or have to leave early one more time to pick up your child from school, you will be fired. Something needs to be done.

The sooner you contact a doctor, the better. The symptoms that accompany your child's ADHD can cause them to be labeled negatively, such as lazy or careless. These labels can follow your child and have a negative impact on their self-esteem.

It's time to make an appointment with a doctor. However, before you do that, find out how many other cases of ADHD the doctor has successfully diagnosed and treated. If your regular doctor has only diagnosed a couple of cases, you might consider taking your child to a specialist, such as a psychologist, developmental pediatrician, etc., who will have a lot of experience diagnosing and working with children who suffer from ADHD.

In most cases, you will not want to work with a general practitioner. One reason is because the testing process and analysis takes several hours. The general practitioner will not usually have enough time to devote to the actions required to determine whether your child has ADHD.

Note that there is a chance that ADHD is accompanied by another diagnosis, such anxiety, bipolar, or oppositional disorder. Specialists will usually test for those issues as well. Your child's regular doctor can recommend a specialist, and so can your insurance provider.

You found the right doctor. So, what's next for you and your child?

The doctor will first determine whether your child has the symptoms of ADHD that the DSM-5 lists. The manual states that your child has to exhibit six of the nine symptoms before the age of twelve. The symptoms have to interfere in at least two of the following settings: home, school, or work.

If the doctor determines that your child does meet the requirements, they will administer a clinical interview that uses a standard ADHD rating scale. This interview and scale will be used to determine whether your child has other issues, such as autism, learning disorders, anxiety, and mood disorders in addition to or other than ADHD.

Evaluation

The first part of the evaluation could take considerable time. It could last anywhere from 45 minutes to two hours or even longer. During this time, the doctor will look for symptoms of ADHD, as well as indications that your child might be suffering from other issues causing the same symptoms. Your child could be asked to take intelligence and memory recall tests during this time.

When you first visit the doctor, make sure you are specific about the issues your child is having. For example, if they are unable to sit still during silent reading time at school, have frequent bursts of anger sometimes for no reason, and if they constantly lose track of everything.

Make sure you know ahead of time what stance you will take on medication and let the doctor know ahead of time. If the doctor insists upon medication, then don't be afraid to find a different one.

There is a lot of paperwork that will need to be filled out, so bring your favorite pen and reading glasses. There are questionnaires, ADHD rating scales, and other checklists to be filled out. Your child's teachers, daycare providers, babysitters, and other people who care for them will be asked to fill out paperwork as well. The more information provided to the doctor, the better because it will help them come up with a more accurate diagnosis.

Your child will also get a physical, which includes a hearing and sight exam, to make sure there are no physical issues causing problems.

Then, the doctor will look at your social history to determine whether there are any other issues that could be causing some of the symptoms, specifically anxiety. Moving around a lot, suffering from money problems, having a family member who is suffering from health problems can all create anxiety. These types of problems can cause your child to exhibit symptoms that are similar to those of ADHD.

Because ADHD is genetic, the doctor will also want to know about your family history. If neither you nor your partner suffers from ADHD, then it is less likely that your child will. If one of you struggles with the mental illness, then your child will have a 50 percent chance of suffering from it as well. There is a significant chance that your child will suffer from ADHD if both their parents also struggle with ADHD.

The doctor will also look at the symptom history. As mentioned, the child has to exhibit a minimum of six of the nine symptoms of impulsiveness, inattentiveness, and/or hyperactivity before they are 12 years old.

You won't receive an instant diagnosis. This isn't an issue where the doctor can do an MRI and see the tumor or other issues that are causing the ADHD. All of the information will be thoroughly examined. Then you will receive a diagnosis. It could take two weeks to receive the information. Meanwhile, inform the teachers and other people involved in your child's life about the progress.

After Diagnosis

If you have decided that medication is an option for your child, you should know that you might have to experiment with different types of drugs and different doses to figure out what will work best for your child.

Have a conversation with the doctor about the different medications and options for your child, as well as potential side effects. You will want to know how the doctor will evaluate whether the medication is working and how it will affect your child.

You will also want to talk about other treatments for your child, such as cognitive behavioral therapy or behavior therapy. You will also want to talk about regular follow up visits to analyze the effectiveness of the medication.

AFTERWORD

Although a diagnosis of ADHD might seem difficult to hear, it will actually help you understand your child and his behaviors easier. Instead of thinking that your child is lazy or bad, you understand that he has a mental illness. The good news is that now you know why your child acts the way he does, you can help them overcome the negative behaviors and be successful in school and in their personal life.

Chapter Summary

- ADHD isn't a diagnosis of negative behavior; it is a mental illness.
- There are many symptoms of ADHD.
- Getting a diagnosis overnight won't happen. However, once a diagnosis is made, there are many ways you can help your child.

In the next chapter, you will learn about medication and other treatment options for ADHD.

CHAPTER TWO: TREATMENTS—MEDICINAL AND THERAPY

*A*lthough there is no cure for ADHD, there are several treatments and coping methods available for your child. Many times, ADHD can be successfully managed through the use of stimulant and nonstimulant medication. The National Institute of Mental Health says that it is important to include other treatments in addition to the medication.

Medication

It is essential that you work with your child's doctor to determine whether medication would be a good option for them. If it is, then you have to work together to decide what type of medication would be best. You also have to determine when the medication should be taken. For example, some parents might decide that their children should only have the medication for school, whereas others might want their children to have the medication during evenings and weekends as well.

Consistency is a very important part of helping your child be successful if you and your child's doctor decides that medication is the right avenue. The directions for the medication should be followed exactly. It is hard to determine whether the medication is working well if it is given sporadically. It is also hard to determine what side effects the medication is causing—if any—if the medication isn't administered at the same time each day.

If there are any concerns about the medication, it is extremely important to contact the doctor immediately.

Stimulants

The most commonly prescribed drugs for ADHD are central nervous system stimulants. They increase dopamine and norepinephrine.

Dopamine is a chemical—a neurotransmitter produced by your brain —that sends messages to and from nerve cells. It also affects how you feel pleasure. In addition, it helps you focus on tasks and make plans. It helps you think, aim for your goals, and find life interesting.

Norepinephrine is also a neurotransmitter produced in your brain. Like dopamine, it sends messages to and from your cells. It is a stress hormone released into your blood when your body senses that there is a stressful event occurring. The chemical increases your heart rate, releases sugar into your blood for more energy, and increases blood flow to your muscles to prepare you for your fight or flight syndrome. It increases your alertness and affects your reaction time. It can affect your mood and ability to concentrate well. Low levels of this particular hormone can cause ADHD.

The stimulants can help your child focus better. Some of the more known stimulants include Adderall and Ritalin.

There are side effects for the stimulants, such as headaches, nervousness, insomnia, dry mouth, weight loss, and irritability. Although they do not occur often, other side affects could be hallucinations, allergic reactions, thoughts of suicide or self-harm, and high blood pressure.

Nonstimulants

Sometimes, your doctor may want to consider nonstimulants as an option to treat the ADHD, especially if the stimulants were ineffective or if your child suffered from serious side effects. The nonstimulants increase norepinephrine levels, which helps improve your child's memory and ability to pay attention. Strattera and Pamelor are part of this group. There are other drugs included in the nonstimulant category, and although doctors don't completely understand how they work, they do affect memory and attention.

The main side effects with nonstimulants are very similar to stimulants. Your child may be cranky, have higher blood pressure, experience weight loss, have a dry mouth, be nervous, have insomnia, or have headaches. In rarer occasions, nonstimulants may cause your child to have seizures, have suicidal thoughts, or practice self-harm, including trying to take their own life.

Nonmedicinal ADHD Treatment Options

There are a lot of options you can try, either in place of or in addition to medicinal treatments. You can work with your doctor to figure out which option might be beneficial.

Psychotherapy

Sometimes, it might be hard for your child to talk about their challenges with ADHD, such as problems with peers, adults, and authority figures. Psychotherapy can give them a chance to talk to someone about these issues and learn how to deal with their relationships better. Many times, this will be done through play therapy, emotional facilitation, and parent coaching.

This therapy type may also help your child examine how they behave and learn how to make better choices for themselves. If there are problems at home, family therapy can help the family learn how to cope with the disruptive behaviors.

Psychotherapy can help people with ADHD decrease their impulsive behaviors. It can help them learn to handle their tendency to be easily distracted. It can also help improve their ability to concentrate on tasks.

The therapist can help your child learn to control their impulsiveness by not reacting immediately and emotionally to situations. Impulsiveness results from behaving automatically and without any thought. In a situation, there is a trigger and then a reaction, and that reaction is usually not good. An example is if the teacher tells your child to put away their toy and they mouth off to them. Psychotherapy can help your child recognize that they are mad and to stop and think about what they are about to say before they talk back.

Procrastination is another negative behavior that the therapist can help your child manage. One method is to ask them how difficult they believe that a certain activity will be. Then, after the activity is completed, they will be asked whether it is as hard as they thought it would be.

Another way that psychotherapy will help your child be more successful is to help them change their mindset about getting specific tasks completed. For example, instead of dreading the essay they have to write, they can think about how happy and relieved they will feel once the assignment is completed.

Psychotherapy would help your child focus on their gifts and strengths. They can think about what they do well. This helps build your child's self confidence and become more successful.

Cognitive Behavior Therapy

The purpose of cognitive behavior therapy (CBT) is to help your child replace negative thoughts, feelings, and actions, with more positive ones. For example, if your child has a learning disability and struggles with math, they might say "I'm stupid and I'll never pass this math class." Cognitive behavior therapy can help them recognize these negative thoughts and replace them with "I struggle with math, but I'm smart enough to figure it out."

In addition to changing negative emotions and actions, it can help improve his abilities to control his behavior. Therapists will help your child learn to adapt to different situations he might encounter. In addition, CBT can help your child become a better problem solver.

Cognitive behavior therapy—which is a talk therapy—uses several techniques to help your child learn to manage the symptoms of their ADHD, such as modeling and roleplaying, so your child can examine their thoughts, feelings, and behaviors, and then restructure them. This type of therapy is used for various mental health issues, such as with depression, anxiety, and self-esteem.

The therapist will work with you and your child to identify problems and challenges they face, set goals, and monitor the process your child is making toward reaching their goals.

First, the therapist will meet with you and your child. They will learn about the issues your child is facing and what they hope to accomplish through therapy sessions. Then, they will work with you to determine how best to help your child.

Modeling is one method that could be used. Modeling is a great way for your child to see the desired behavior. For example, the therapist might model what it looks like to raise their hand in class when they want to speak.

Roleplaying is another method that could be used. The therapist could pretend to be your child and your child can then see their behavior through the eyes of their teacher. Then, they can be the teacher when the correct behavior is used.

Cognitive restructuring is another technique that the therapist can use to help your child. This method helps your child recognize when they are having negative thoughts and replace them with positive ones.

All of these techniques can help your child monitor their own behavior. They can notice when they are being restless or speaking out of turn, and then change the course of their actions. It will help them develop plans and implement those plans to overcome challenges or reach specific goals. In addition, it will help them be aware of continuous positive and negative reinforcement for their actions.

The therapy sessions may be one on one with a therapist or conducted as a group session. The therapist might also give your child "homework" to do between sessions, such as monitoring their negative thoughts, feelings, and actions, what provoked them, and what they did to change them.

Cognitive behavior therapy is shorter than most types of therapy. They usually last between ten and 20 sessions.

There are some cautions about this type of therapy. One is that it might not work for younger children because your child has to be old enough to recognize and understand their thought patterns. Some children are able to do this when they are six or seven years old. However, some children struggle with this, even when they are older.

The other caution about this type of therapy is that it seems to work more on issues that accompany ADHD, such as depression, anxiety, etc., as opposed to ADHD.

ADHD Coaching

ADHD coaches are trained to help people who suffer from ADHD to manage their lives better. A coach could help your child develop important life skills that could help them be more successful at home, with their peers, and at school.

One skill that the coach can help your child learn is planning. It might be easy for them to set a goal. For example, their goal is to earn at least a B in their math class. However, planning how they will achieve that goal might be more difficult, as it requires them to think long term, which can be difficult for them because of their ADHD. In addition, managing their time, work, and other skills needed to achieve each step of their goal could be daunting.

Their coach could also help them improve their self-esteem. With each success they achieve, their self-confidence and self-efficacy (the belief that they are capable of achieving their goals) will also increase. This will also increase their motivation.

The coach can also help them improve relationships with their family, friends, and other people in their life. They will have better judgment regarding their own behavior, relationships, and academics.

If you believe that an ADHD coach would benefit your child, then it is important to find the right life skills coach. First, you need to make sure the coach is an ADHD coach. There is no specific certification that coaches need to have to be considered an ADHD coach; however, there is training that they go through offered by many universities that often has specific criteria that defines an ADHD coach. To find a coach who specializes in working with people who suffer from ADHD, you can look for those recommended by the ADHD Coaching Organization. This organization screens life coaches to determine whether they have the appropriate training before the coaches are listed on the *List of Professional ADHD Coaches.*

It is important to remember that an ADHD coach isn't a therapist or a psychiatrist. The coach's goal is to help your child achieve specific goals to help him deal with his ADHD symptoms better.

Once you have found the right coach who can help your child achieve their goals, then you will have your initial meeting with the coach. This is the time that the coach will get to know your child and figure out what strategies are already or have been used in the past. The coaches will talk about the biggest problems that you and your child want to solve, as well as what you and your child would like to accomplish.

Then, your coach will work with you to determine what steps need to be taken to help your child achieve their goals. The coach will then give him an assignment, which your child and their coach will review during the second session.

There are several questions that the coach might ask your child during their second session. One is what did you accomplish that you wanted to accomplish? Another question is what goal did you not accomplish and why? Then, the coach will talk to your child about strategies that they could use to avoid the barriers to accomplishing set goals. Finally, the coach will ask you and your child what you would like to work on for the rest of the session.

You and your child should discuss what kind of support you would like from the coach, such as phone calls, text messages, or no contact between sessions.

The coach should help your child celebrate their successes, such as accomplishing goals that your child might have been intimidated by. The coach should also work with your child to find out why certain goals aren't being met, and then work to find a strategy that will help your child to achieve their goals.

Your child might show progress after one session. The progress might be small, such as cleaning their room or staying in their chair for an entire lesson. Progress will continue but may lag after a while. At this point, your child and coach may have to develop new goals or strategies, or it might be time to find a new coach.

The coach will give you a plan at the beginning of each session. They will give your child a different way of looking at the mistakes they made between sessions. If your child had a bad week, then the coach can help them analyze those feelings, then discuss what your child did that was positive or what goals they accomplished.

One way to determine whether the coaching is accomplishing your combined goals and if your child is able to accomplish tasks that they previously found overwhelming. This is important because it means the coach has helped empower your child to find and use the strengths and abilities that they had all along to be successful.

Most of the time, ADHD coaching doesn't last a long time. The goal of ADHD coaching is to help your child change how they perceive themselves and empower them to use their strengths to be successful. They are taught how to coach themselves.

Once the coach has helped your child incorporate the strategies learned into their everyday life, then regular sessions probably aren't necessary. However, your child can always call upon the coach for help after the sessions have ended for advice.

Behavior Therapy

Behavior therapy is often combined with medication as a treatment plan for kids who have ADHD, although some people choose behavior therapy without medication. It is important to determine which avenue is right for you.

Behavior therapy isn't a cure for ADHD, nor does it affect any of the symptoms that your child may suffer from as a result of ADHD. It also doesn't change how their brain will function. However, there are many benefits to behavior therapy.

Behavior problems that result from ADHD can be addressed by restructuring their time at home. It helps address negative behavior by establishing routines and a sense of organization and predictability. It increases the amount of positive attention you give your child. It is based on common sense parenting.

Behavior therapy designed to help your child with their ADHD consists of four components. One is that it teaches you to reinforce your child's good behavior with a reward system. You would ignore negative behavior, unless it is too bad to ignore. Then, they would face appropriate consequences, such as losing rewards, privileges, or having a timeout. In addition, behavior therapy can help you recognize and remove anything that triggers your child's negative behavior.

This type of therapy can help your child manage any negative behaviors that cause stress and problems in their home and school life. The goal of behavior therapy is to develop positive behaviors and eliminate the negative ones. The therapist will teach your child different strategies they can use to improve their focus, organization, and impulsiveness.

They will learn better skills to help them pay attention in class, complete homework, and do their chores.

It is important that your child learns to understand and monitor their own behavior if they are to make positive changes. Not only will that make them more successful as a student, but also as an adult. Behavior therapy is a good way to teach them these skills.

The therapist will work with you and your child to set goals for them. Then, the therapist will help you use certain techniques at home.

While you are working with the therapist, you will examine how you handle your child's negative behaviors because sometimes, the way you react to the negative behavior could unintentionally reinforce their bad actions. You'll learn why some techniques aren't working to help your child's behavior improve. Then, you will learn new strategies that will be more effective.

Your therapist can help you work with your child to examine how they behave in certain situations. Then, together, you can develop strategies in response, such as direct feedback. A reward system may also be a solution. If there are behavior problems at school, then it might be a good idea to get their teacher involved in creating solutions.

You encourage your child's positive behavior by rewarding them. This could be free time, a special activity, toy, or whatever item or privilege they want. By the same token, you can take away the reward when there is negative behavior.

The reward system is a way to teach your child that it is important to follow the rules and there are consequences if those rules are not followed. In other words, the purpose of behavior modification therapy is to help your child learn that certain behaviors have consequences. This, in turn, will help them control their impulses in engaging in those negative behaviors.

It is essential that you determine which behaviors are acceptable and which are intolerable. You have to stick with your boundaries. Punishing a behavior one day and not punishing it another will only confuse your child and harm their growth. They won't know which behaviors are allowed and which are not.

There are some behaviors that should also be considered unacceptable, such as refusing to get out of bed or go to bed when told, having physical outbursts, or refusing other requests, such as turning off video games, picking up their mess, etc.

The rules should be made very clear to your child. You should put them as simply as you can and write down important rules where your child can see them.

Following the rules should be rewarded. If they turn off their video game when you first request it, then they can get a small treat or be rewarded points for a bigger prize, such as money, a night at the movies, or a new video game or toy they have been wanting.

Sometimes, you can ignore behavior that is mildly disruptive because it might be a way for them to blow off steam or release some of that energy that has been building up inside of them. However, any kind of abusive, violent, willfully disruptive, or destructive behavior should be dealt with. Punishment can include the removal of rewards, such as taking points away from a goal or grounding them from technology or game systems.

Process of Behavior Therapy

When you first meet with a therapist, you'll talk about your goals for your child. Together, you will identify which of their behaviors are the most problematic. Then, you will develop a plan that can help you and your child improve their behavior.

The behavior modification plan consists of developing a reward and consequence system. You will create a chart that shows your child how they can meet their targeted goals to earn rewards. The rewards are selected by your child, so they will be privileges, toys, or other items that he will really want to work for.

An example of a behavior that you will put on the chart is that your child will not disrupt their class during silent reading. Their teacher will send a note or initial their planner when your child meets this goal. At home, you can record points on the chart. Once your child has five days of not disrupting class, they can have an extra half hour of playing their video games.

If they do disrupt the class during this time, they simply won't earn a point. That is the consequence, thus additional punishments should not be administered.

You and the therapist will meet weekly to talk about the chart and any problems that have come up.

Your child will meet with the therapist monthly. The therapist will help them develop skills that can help them successfully earn points on the chart. Your child will also learn methods they can use to help them meet their goals both at school and home. The therapist will also help them acquire new strategies that will help them handle their anger issues and increase their ability to control their actions.

Is It Working?

Unfortunately, there is no written test that can help you easily determine whether the lessons learned from the behavior therapy are working. However, there are several ways you and the therapist can figure out whether behavior therapy is effective.

The chart is one great tool. If your child is earning a lot of points for positive behavior, then that is an indication that the therapy is working. In addition, fewer phone calls from the teacher complaining about your child's classroom behavior would be an indication that their behavior at school has improved. Another indication that the behavior therapy is working is if they struggle less with issues at school, appear to be less frustrated, and if their confidence has increased.

If the behavior therapy isn't working, then another system would need to be developed, such as taking away points on the chart for unacceptable behavior. Meanwhile, the therapist will continue working with your child to help them develop strategies to manage issues that accompany ADHD.

. . .

Behavior Therapy at School

A lot of times, the negative behavior manifests itself at school, so it is important that you work with the school and your child's teacher. The teacher can monitor your child's behavior in the problematic areas and report back to you about whether your child is achieving their goals.

One way that the teacher can help your child is to set up a chart for school. The teacher can mark off which of the goals your child has successfully accomplished. If they have accomplished a certain number of these tasks, then they can earn points on their chart at home.

Social Skills Training

One of the problems that kids with ADHD face is knowing how to behave in social settings. They might not understand social cues, such as facial expressions, figurative language, sarcasm, different voice tones, etc. This means they might not know how to respond appropriately to their peers. Many children who suffer from ADHD tend to be more aggressive, which can cause them to face rejection often.

Children who suffer from ADHD might be unable to start conversations and then, when conversations are started, they cannot sustain them. They may not understand non-verbal cues, such as body language.

Social skills training can help your child learn new ways to work and play with others and better behaviors when in a social setting. During this type of therapy, they might learn how to share toys and wait their turn during games. He might also learn how to ask for help when he needs it. In addition, he can learn coping skills if he is teased by other people.

During this training, the therapist might model appropriate social interactions. They might teach your child how to increase their self-awareness and keep track of their behaviors. Your child will learn how to improve their problem solving and anger management skills. They will also learn how to have appropriate conversations with other people.

One important skill that your child would learn during social skills training is to not believe that every action or comment made by others is negative. This, in turn, will help them control their angry responses.

Social skills training seems to be more effective when it is done in a group setting. This is because children have a harder time seeing their own behavior than seeing other people act out positive and negative behaviors.

The groups in social skills training are usually small and consist of no more than two to eight children. The group is led by a therapist who helps the children learn how to have good conversations with their peers, as well as how to form friendships and develop good problem solving skills. In addition, during these sessions, the therapists teach the children how to control their emotions. The children also learn how to recognize and understand issues and situations through other people's perspectives.

During this type of therapy, your child will learn important skills that they will use for the rest of their life. One skill is how to greet other people. They will learn how to start and sustain a conversation once it is started. They will also learn how to respond to other people effectively. Social skills training will teach them how to share their toys and other resources. In addition, they will learn how to take turns, either during the learning process or play time. Social skills training will also help your child learn how to ask for help when they need it.

Research suggests that parent training can improve the success of social skills training. Peer mentors may also help.

Like cognitive behavior therapy, the effectiveness of social skills training seems to be somewhat limited. One reason is because children are generally unable to apply specific skills to various situations.

Parent Child Interaction Therapy

Parent child interaction therapy (PCIT) is an evidenced based therapy that was developed at the University of Florida. This therapy focuses on the relationship between you and your preschool-aged child. The purpose of this therapy is to improve dysfunctional relationships between you and your child, as well as decrease negative behavior issues that younger children, who suffer from ADHD, may often display. This includes oppositional defiant disorder.

This therapy method has two phases. The therapist facilitates effective and positive discipline by helping improve the positive relationship between you and your child. This can then help you develop a nurturing and positive atmosphere in which the therapy will take place.

Child directed interaction (CDI) takes place in this first stage. During this stage, you will interact with your child positively and reinforce them. You will avoid giving commands, asking questions, or criticizing your child as you play.

Parent directed interaction (PDI) happens after you have mastered the skills taught during phase one, which will be designed to make the attachment relationship stronger. In this stage, you will give direct, clear, and concise commands to your child. In addition, you will practice setting limits. You will practice giving timeouts to your child if they disobey your instructions or overstep their boundaries, while also praising them when they do obey.

For both stages of this therapy, you would wear an earpiece through which the therapist—who is watching the interactions behind a one-way mirror—can coach you on how to use the new skills you have learned.

There are no set limits for the number of therapy sessions you and your child will attend. The therapy will continue until both you and your child have mastered the skills necessary, and your child demonstrates a significant decrease in their negative behavior.

This therapy method has been proven to be effective for even years after the therapy sessions have ended. Research has shown that PCIT may have a direct impact on the symptoms that accompany ADHD. This means that your child may not be as hyperactive, and that they may be less aggressive and have improved relationships with their peers. In addition, it could potentially decrease the need for medication.

Music Therapy

Music has been shown to help people with ADHD to focus, increase their ability to pay attention, and reduce hyperactive behavior. Music also helps these people improve their social skills.

Music helps your child's brain to stay on a linear path because music has structure. The structure is the rhythm of the music. It has a very definite beginning, middle, and end, which helps people with ADHD plan their actions, anticipate events, problems, or other issues, and then react to them, according to Kirsten Hutchison, who is a music therapist at Music Works Northwest.

According to research studies, music can help synapses fire up. Dopamine is increased when pleasurable music is played. Dopamine, which helps regulate attention, working memory, and motivation, is low in people who suffer from ADHD. Patti Catalano, a neurologic music therapist at Music Works Northwest, said, "Music shares neural networks with other cognitive processes. Through brain imaging, we can see how music lights up the left and right lobes. The goal of music therapy is to build up those activated brain muscles over time to help overall function."

Music therapy often requires your child to work with other people to write songs and play an instrument, practicing for a performance. Music is social because if one person, instrument, or voice is missing, then the entire song changes. Because music is a social concept, music therapy can greatly help your child learn to listen, take turns, anticipate changes, and even pick up on cues that they might have struggled with before.

Benefits

Music helps your child improve their attention and concentration. The rhythm and tempo of the music can help mitigate some of the symptoms of ADHD. Learning to play an instrument can help your child increase their ability to pay attention for longer periods of time, as well as control their impulses and improve their decision-making skills. Music can help improve the auditory connections in the brain, which ADHD can diminish. An added bonus is that music can help train your child to function well in a noisy environment, which is an important life skill.

In addition, music helps reinforce your child's memory. There is a reason that little children can often sing 26 letters before they can recite ten numbers. Music helps people remember information.

Music can help your child keep track of time. When they are doing chores to a certain playlist, they know when their time is about up. Music with a fast tempo and rhythm can also help increase energy, whereas slower music can help calm your child down.

An important benefit of music is that it can increase self-esteem. Learning songs and how to play an instrument can help your child feel a sense of accomplishment. They can then feel proud that they have learned to play or sing. It also teaches your child that practice is important, and that it is important to keep trying, even if they aren't successful at first.

As discussed, children who suffer from ADHD often have difficulty making friends and maintaining relationships. However, music is a great way to establish those relationships, since it is something that almost everyone has in common. If your child plays an instrument and is involved in a band, then these bonds will be even stronger.

You can use music as a reward. Once they get their homework and chores done, they can listen to music. Buying certain music could also be rewards that they can strive for and earn with good behavior.

Music can also help your child express their thoughts and feelings. It helps them examine what is going on inside of themselves. Writing songs is a great way to express those thoughts and feelings and share them with others.

In addition to teaching your child how to examine their own thoughts and feelings, it can also teach him to understand the perceptions of other people. They can learn empathy by listening to others' thoughts and feelings.

When Formal Music Therapy Isn't an Option

So, you are financially tapped out. Music therapy sounds great, but you just don't have the resources. There are ways your child can benefit from music anyway.

One way is to change the channels on the television. Instead of watching their favorite television show, you can put on some Beethoven or other calming music. Change the music with different activities. For chores, perhaps some rock and roll would help trigger the brain to move. Beethoven during homework might help them focus. You should experiment with different types of music to determine what helps them best.

Songs with different tempos will trigger your child's brain to move at different tempos. Upbeat, fast-paced music would be a good option when your child needs to move physically and accomplish tasks. Put on some Dep Leppard while they are helping do chores around the house. Some Mozart while reading a book at bedtime might help your child sleep.

Rebecca West, who works with the Music Institute of Chicago said, "Rhythm, melody, and tempo are tools used to target non-musical behaviors, to catapult change throughout the body. A change in rhythm can trigger a reaction in the brain. 'Oooh, something's changed; I need to pay attention!' You can bring down the tempo to spur slower movements, or bring up the melody to trigger pleasure."

Another way to use music to help your child is to have a playlist that corresponds with the chart of duties you have created for them. For example, you could have a group of songs that you play every morning to help them know when they need to accomplish certain tasks. *Carry on My Wayward Son* could be their signal to get out of bed, go to the bathroom, comb their hair, and wash their face. *Living on a Prayer* would signal that it's time to get dressed and head out to the kitchen for breakfast. Then, the song, *We Will Rock You* tells them that it is time to brush their teeth. These songs are just examples; feel free to switch them up to your and your child's tastes.

Concetta Tomaino, the executive director for the Institute for Music Neurologic Function, said, "Music facilitates multi-step processing when executive-function deficits may make it difficult."

Tomaino suggested using a drum can help your child learn how to take turns. She said that you should play a beat on a drum and say a phrase while doing it. Then, your child will repeat it. After them, it is your turn again, only this time, you should add a beat and some words. She said, "I'm asking him to listen, pay attention, and control his impulses. I'm also showing him that his turn is worth waiting for."

It is also important to listen to your child and his preferences for music. Although you might prefer the more classical sounds of Beethoven and Mozart when studying, reading, or working, your child might do better with KISS. It is important to let them listen to the music they prefer, as long as they are getting their tasks accomplished.

Art Therapy

When people hear the word "art," their minds almost always go to *The Last Supper* by Leonardo da Vinci, or the ceiling of the Sistine Chapel painted by Michelangelo. However, art is a lot more than that. It is the act of creating something. Although your child may not be the next Picasso, they can still reap significant rewards from art therapy.

Art therapy can be an important technique that can help your child. It would help them learn to handle their impulsiveness, increase their ability to make positive decisions, and increase their coping mechanisms. It would also help them improve their organization and sequencing. It helps them learn to be flexible and improve their social skills.

The art allows your child to express their thoughts and feelings through visual images that they create through drawing, painting, sculpting, or other art exercises. This can be especially important for those who have a difficult time talking about their thoughts and feelings.

Art therapy has an added bonus for those with ADHD because creating art means they are constantly moving. It can help your child create a mental and emotional focus that they might be unable to have during regular talk therapy.

Because thoughts and feelings are constantly bombarding your child's brain, they might have trouble finding the word that would help them express their challenges. After all, if their forgetfulness and impulsiveness are frustrating to you and their teacher, you know that these issues definitely agitate your child. It can be hard enough for an adult to find the right words to discuss their own frustrations; it would be even harder for a child, especially a young one. Art therapy can help your child express these irritations, which can be helpful for your child who struggles to organize their thoughts in a way that makes sense to them, let alone the people they are trying to communicate with. According to Michael Fogel, a board certified art psychotherapist at the Child & Family Art Center in Pennsylvania, said that artwork helps people understand what your child is feeling and thinking. He called art a bridge that links you to their inner world. The art tells the story of your child's coping skills, how they handle stress, and any other conflicts and emotions they are dealing with.

Fogel said that creating art is more than just a way for your child to communicate; it is also therapeutic. Even the process of choosing which medium they will use and handling that medium can help your child.

Mr. Fogel stated that different art materials have various qualities and structures. "More structured materials are easier to control, a pencil has a fine point, which lends the user a lot of internal controls." This type of art medium will help your child have more control over themselves and be less impulsive. If your child doesn't have a lot of control over their behavior or emotions, using an art tool such as a pencil can help them focus on learning that control.

Art material such as clay, pastels, and paint are messy, not as structured, and can be more difficult to control. Fogel said, "These messy things actually tend to loosen up people's internal controls, and sometimes you may want that if you're trying to dig for feelings or explore concepts and trauma."

According to Mr. Fogel, "Kids with ADHD can feel out of control because their behaviors and habits have been out of their control." Art therapy helps your child practice that self control. The therapist can ask your child to paint something. Then, if it turns out to be a huge mess, the therapist can ask them how their project turned out and whether they are satisfied with it. Afterwards, the therapist can ask them to consider what they would do differently that could make their project turn out better. Art therapy provides structure for your child.

Art can also help your child think about predicting consequences and cause and effect. These concepts are usually challenging to people who suffer from ADHD.

Sequential thinking would also be difficult for your child because they are so easily distracted. Art would help your child stay focused and consider the next steps they should take logically.

Art therapy will help your child's brain develop. Mr. Fogel said, "We have found that when you stimulate the brain and practice and use it, the brain develops more connections, and so by simply doing something in the external world and repeating and rehearsing, there's an outside/ inside connection. So with art therapy, the brain is learning to adapt and translate those learned experiences into everyday life, helping the person make better decisions at school and at home."

Creating art helps stimulate the brain. This stimulation is very important because it helps increase the dopamine levels in your child's brain, which, in turn, can help them stay focused, not only on their art project, but on other tasks as well.

Equine Assisted Therapy

Tons of young children dream of having a horse when they are little. Horses are beautiful, majestic animals that are a part of almost every fairy-tale ever written. Horses are known to have many uses, as they race and pull plows and romantic carriages. However, horses have an additional benefit for those with ADHD.

Natural Lifemanship is an equine assisted therapy (EAP) technique that has been proven to help children who suffer from ADHD. It focuses on forming healthy relationships. Horses are very particular about how they interact with humans, and in order for a good relationship to be formed, there must be trust and mutual respect between the animal and child.

One important aspect of Natural Lifemanship is that your child would learn to detect and understand nonverbal cues, a skill that many children with ADHD lack. Horses provide immediate feedback to your child's actions, which is something that humans don't always do.

To form a healthy relationship with a horse, your child must learn to recognize and control the chaos that exists inside of themselves. Then, they can learn to detect and mitigate the chaos that exists externally.

Deb Huber, a licensed professional counselor in Pennsylvania who helps some of her clients through Natural Lifemanship, states that equine therapy can help increase focus, self-control, and improve social skills. In addition, people with ADHD who work with horses improve their ability to control their impulses. Their communication skills improve, as does their empathy, trust, and confidence.

. . .

Alternative Therapy

There are a lot of other therapy methods that many doctors and people have tried. Some of them are a bit controversial, not because they are dangerous, but because there is some debate about their effectiveness. Whether you should look into these methods should be a discussion between you, your partner, your child, and your child's doctor.

Endeavor Rx

Endeavor Rx is a video game designed to help treat people with cognitive disabilities. This game, which is FDA-approved and can only be downloaded with a prescription, was created based on research from neuroscientists. The video game was developed to treat cognitive disabilities by targeting the specific sources of the disability in the brain.

The company that created the product said, "Our digital medicine is delivered through creative and immersive video game experiences to keep patients engaged and immersed in the treatment. Our products leverage the fun, deep engagement, and rewards that make them incredibly compelling but, unlike typical video games, this personalized gameplay experience is engineered with adaptive algorithms designed to improve cognitive function."

There are three core technologies designed to help your child with their ADHD symptoms. The first is selective stimulus management engine (SSME). This technology is designed to help improve attention, focus, and memory. The second technology is body brain trainer (BBT), designed to help improve attention and working memory. It also helps them control impulsiveness and manage their goals. Spatial navigation engine (SNAV) is technology that can help your child's ability to determine and sustain the trajectory between two points, such as a basketball to a hoop. The SNAV helps improve memory, organization, and planning.

If you think this option might help your child, then you might want to take some information about the game to your doctor and show them how it might be beneficial for your child. Then, they will need to write a prescription for it. You would hook up with the website and submit the prescription. Then, you can download and pay for the game.

. . .

Chiropractor

There are some people who believe that sending your child to a chiropractor can help them with their ADHD symptoms. There is no research to support that chiropractors can help, so you should talk to your doctor before taking your child to one.

One reason why some believe that chiropractors might make a difference is because there is an imbalance in the child's muscle tone that causes the activity in the brain to be off-balanced. The chiropractor makes spinal adjustments that can help restore balance to their brain. In addition, your child would be exposed to different frequencies of light and sound.

The neural organizational technique—otherwise known as applied kinesiology—is another chiropractic theory for the cause of ADHD. This theory is based on the idea that your child's skull bones have become misaligned, which, in turn, puts unequal pressure on different parts of the brain. This then causes the brain to work improperly.

Neurofeedback

Neurofeedback is a treatment that would teach your child how to change their brain waves so that they would be able to focus better. This treatment is based on the idea that people who suffer from ADHD have more theta waves than others, along with fewer beta waves.

To test your child's brain waves through an electroencephalograph (EEG), your child would have sensors put on their head. These are often put on by a head piece that looks like a bike helmet. These sensors are painless. They do not go into your child's scalp or into their head, and the sensors monitor your child's brain waves through these sensors. A scientist can study the brain waves to determine what patterns are present. The brain makes four waves: alpha, which is a medium wave; beta, a fast wave; theta, a slow wave; and delta, which is when you are in deep sleep.

While wearing the sensors, your child will get to play a game on the computer that they will control with their brain. When the sensors pick up your child's brain waves—which indicate that they are concentrating—it triggers a reward, which could be a sound or movement.

The theory behind this technique is that your child will learn how it feels to concentrate, which, in turn, can help them create more of the brain waves to help with their ADHD symptoms.

The question is whether it works. Some doctors say that it does work, whereas others say that there needs to be more research.

Dr. Naomi Steiner, a developmental and behavioral pediatrician at Boston Medical Center, says that she uses it on her pediatric patients who suffer from ADHD. She said, "Those circuits improve your child's ability to 'switch' on her brain, and focus for longer periods of time. During training, your child is forming new neuronal connections—that is, new circuits in the brain."

Dr. Steiner said that it is an option if your child isn't responding to medication, and it doesn't have any side effects. However, there are still things to consider before deciding to have your child partake in neurofeedback.

1. Your child does not have to stop their medication to participate in this type of treatment.
2. You won't see results right away. For the neurofeedback to be effective, your child will need to see their doctor or therapist weekly for several months.
3. Insurance will not always cover the doctors or treatments. You should check with your insurance company before you decide to try this technique.
4. This is not a technique that just anyone can administer. Only doctors, nurses, therapists, or psychologists who have been specially trained in this type of therapy can work with neurofeedback treatments.

Working Memory Training

Working memory training is another technique that could be helpful for your child. Working memory is defined as remembering information, and then using it within a short time period. It is the short term memory that retains information long enough for them to concentrate on completing a task, and then recall what action is next.

According to Dr. Torkel Klingberg, a professor of cognitive neuroscience at the Karolinska Institute in Stockholm, Sweden, "Working memory is like plastic—flexible, moveable, and trainable, similar to our muscles. It can be improved with 'exercise' and training."

Research indicates that working memory training—or cogmed—can be effective at reducing some of the symptoms associated with ADHD, such as the inability to pay attention, impulsiveness, and hyperactivity.

Cogmed is a user adaptive computer program that you would download to your computer. It is presented in the format of a video game. And what child doesn't love video games? The program has animation and graphics, as well as clear sound.

Once it is downloaded, your child would log into the training website. The program has fifteen exercises for your child to practice with. Then, once he has completed those, he would begin working on the tracked exercises. The tasks become harder because the goal is to help your child increase his ability to concentrate on a specific goal and then achieve it within a specific amount of time.

Dr. Nicole Hraniotis, a psychiatrist, states that you should hire a cogmed trainer to work with your child while they start the training. The trainer will talk with your child at least once a week to figure out how much progress they have made. Then, the trainer will answer any questions you or your child may have.

According to Dr. Hraniotis, people who have used cogmed said that they paid more attention to their environment than they did in the past. They also stated that they were better able to recognize social cues. Children also said that they felt as though they had better control over their actions and emotions. Parents reported that they don't have to harp on their children as much to take care of everyday actions, such as showering or brushing their teeth.

Dr. Hraniotis reported that approximately 75 percent of the children who used cogmed training demonstrated decreased impulsiveness and hyperactivity, along with an increased ability to focus on tasks for longer periods. The training also made significant changes in the participants' brain activity.

She stated, "Although some mental health professionals complain that there is not enough scientific evidence to support the success of cogmed training in the treatment and management of ADHD, current studies disagree with those assertions. In fact, a 2005 study found that after five weeks of cogmed training, ADHD children's memories not only improved, their attention, focus, and concentration also improved. Other studies have yielded similar results."

The great thing about using cogmed or other working memory programs is that there are no negative side effects. Therefore, if it really doesn't help your child as much as you had hoped, then it has caused no harm to your child.

It is important to remember that your child should continue taking their medication, as working memory training is not a substitute for medication or other treatments. Dr. Hraniotis stated that because the tasks can be difficult, she doesn't recommend the program for children younger than eight.

There are also other working memory apps that you can have your child try. If you keep forgetting where you put your keys or phone, you can play the games, as well.

One site is the memory gym. This application features challenges that include flashing numbers, shapes, cards, and words. It also has spoken numbers and counting dots. The program includes tips on how to memorize information.

SharpBrains.com has brain teasers with challenges to help improve memory, attention, math, logic, pattern recognition, and planning.

Vismory is a memory game that even younger children can use to help improve their memory, attention, and planning.

Fit Brains Trainer has more than 300 games. The program is designed to improve your child's processing speed, problem solving skills, concentration, and memory.

Monster hunt is another memory improvement game that everyone in your family can play.

There are a lot more apps available for the computer and on the phone for both you and your child to play. As with all types of apps, some are free, some are low cost, and others cost a little more. You should read reviews from other people who have used the apps to determine which one would be the most beneficial for your child.

AFTERWORD

When a child gets diagnosed with ADHD, the parents' mind almost always goes toward medication. Medication, usually stimulants, are often one of the treatments that your child's doctor will prescribe to help your child be more successful in overcoming the symptoms of their ADHD.

However, there are many other treatment methods that can help your child. Behavior therapy and cognitive behavior therapy are more formal types of treatment that may help. Other types of therapy, such as music therapy, art therapy, and equine assistance therapy may also help them improve their social and organizational skills, along with other functions that can be challenging to children with ADHD.

There are some alternative methods available as well. These methods have not had a lot of studies completed on them, so before you choose to have your child engaged in one of them, you should do a lot of research on them and contact your child's doctor.

Chapter Summary

- Although medication is often used to treat ADHD, there are other options as well.
- Behavior therapy and cognitive behavior therapy are just two types of therapy that can help your child learn to manage the symptoms of their ADHD.

- Other types of therapy, such as music, art, and equine therapy can also help your child manage his symptoms of ADHD and help him be more successful.

In the next chapter, you will learn how your child can learn different types of coping methods to manage their ADHD symptoms and the stress that often accompanies those symptoms.

CHAPTER THREE: WAYS TO HELP YOUR CHILD COPE AND GROW

*R*elaxation helps adults, especially after they've had a rough day and just need a moment of quiet. Kids, especially those with ADHD, can benefit greatly from learning how to relax when there is chaos all around them. There are several relaxation techniques that they can learn from, such as meditation, breathing exercises, yoga, visualizations, mindfulness, among many other techniques. These techniques can help your child understand the connection between their mind, emotions, and body.

Meditation

Most people think of the monks, sitting cross-legged and chanting when they think of meditation. The idea of trying to sit still for long periods can make most people run for the hills. For the ADHD child, the word would make them run twice as fast.

Like all muscles, the brain needs to be exercised. Meditation is one way your child can exercise their brain.

Although it might seem like a silly joke when you are encouraged to have your child engage in meditation practices, many experts agree that meditation is one of the best tools that can help your child. Meditation helps your child slow down and think about situations before they act. It counteracts your child's natural impulse to react to every stimulus without thinking about the situation or consequences.

Erin Snyder, an ADHD parenting educator and coach, said, "In order for your ADHD child to begin to develop the executive function/self-regulation skills she lacks, she must become aware of her thoughts. Meditation or 'mindfulness' is hands-down the number one way to do this."

There are many other benefits to meditating.

Regardless of how your child chooses to meditate, the overall benefits of meditation remain the same.

One benefit is that it helps your child learn to control their attention. Instead of their mind wandering all over the place when they need to be focusing on a task or paying attention to a lesson or conversation, they can learn to concentrate. It also helps them learn to bring their thoughts back to the task at hand when they start to wander. They will learn how to bring their attention and thoughts back to the task at hand, even if there are distractions happening around them.

Another benefit of mindfulness is that it can help reduce the mental and physical hyperactivity that is the hallmark of ADHD.

Meditation can also help your child connect with their thoughts and emotions, which in turn helps them become less impulsive. This then can reduce defiant behavior that is a result of impulsive reactions they may have.

Dopamine levels are increased when you meditate. Some research suggests that this can actually reduce the need for medication.

The prefrontal cortex of your child's brain will be thickened when they meditate. This part of their brain is in charge of focusing on tasks, planning, and controlling his impulses.

Meditation practices also decrease anxiety and depression, which is common among people who suffer from ADHD. Meditation also helps reduce stress, which can cause anxiety and depression.

The practice lowers the number of stress hormones, such as cortisol, even when they are in situations that would normally cause them to feel anxious.

Your child's self-esteem might increase as he meditates, because meditation can help them redirect negative thoughts and turn them into more positive ones.

Talk to your child about their thoughts and feelings before and after they meditate. How do they feel before they start? How do they feel after they have completed their meditation? Recognizing the answers to these questions will help them connect the practice with a change in their thoughts and emotions.

Myths

Although some people do sit when they meditate, there are other ways to meditate that allow you to stand or even move. You can meditate while walking or running.

There is no right or wrong way to meditate. There are many forms of meditation that your child can engage in.

Their brain does not have to be completely quiet to meditate. In fact, it is practically impossible to completely shut down all thoughts that bounce around inside anyone's brain.

Another myth about meditation is that it has to go on for certain time periods. In fact, a person can successfully meditate for one minute to multiple hours.

Meditation also doesn't have to be done in silence. Your child can learn to meditate while listening to music, humming, singing, etc.

Another common misconception about meditation is that it is hard, yet people meditate unconsciously all the time. The point of meditating for your child would be to do so specifically to concentrate on a thought or feeling. It is about connecting with themselves.

Best Practices for All Meditation Methods

Your child needs to be comfortable when they begin to meditate. Many meditation coaches say that people who are meditating shouldn't be so comfortable that they fall asleep; however, if your child does fall asleep while meditating, then they likely need the rest.

They should get into a position that is most comfortable for them, whether it is lying down on their bed or hanging upside down from a tree branch outside.

Slow, even breaths are essential for successful meditation, although breathing techniques may vary depending on the technique.

If they have a certain time at which they want to meditate, then they might need to schedule some specific time to wind down. It's very difficult for someone who is sprinting to come to a dead stop. They might listen to some soothing music, take a shower, or some other activity that can help them transition from high speed to calm.

You might consider meditating with your child too. This can help them feel more comfortable and focused.

How to Get Your Child Started

Modeling meditation practices is the first step in getting your child interested in meditating. Children, especially younger ones, are always interested in what their parents are doing. Many times, they will want to do exactly what you are doing. So, when you sit quietly for a couple of minutes and focus on your breathing, your child may be curious. They will ask questions. What are you doing? Why are you doing that? Then, they might be interested enough to try it with you.

The second step is to find a place where you and your child can meditate. It could be somewhere in the house or a favorite walking trail.

Children's attention spans are short. When your child has ADHD, it's even shorter. Therefore, you should start with one minute for every year of their age. However, you should still also play it by ear because trying to get a ten-year-old to focus for ten minutes, especially right off the bat, could be like trying to teach your dog to play the piano.

Don't have any specific expectations for either you or your child. They might not stay still. You might not stay still. Their preferred pose might be hanging upside down from the monkey bars. All of that is okay.

Provide something for your child to focus on while they are meditating. It could be a candle flame, the clouds, or even a favorite toy.

Rewards for meditating never hurt. After meditating for a full week, you could have a family night where you make popcorn and watch a movie or play board games. You could put out a jar and have them fill it with macaroni noodles, marbles, or some other token. Then, when the jar is full, they can be rewarded with a pizza night, ice cream, or some other reward of their choice.

The true goal is to encourage your child to meditate and help them find ways to control their thoughts, concentration, and impulsive behaviors.

Meditation Methods for Your Child with ADHD

Book Walking

This is also a technique that all your children can get involved in. Basically, your child would put a book on their head. The goal is to walk a specific path—either inside the house or outside—with a book on their head, without letting the book fall. Their entire focus is on the book and making sure it stays put. Because they are concentrating on the book, the chaos in their brain will have slowed.

Maze Walking

This is a meditation method that can be done inside or outside. If it is a nice day out, grab a piece of chalk and draw a curved line or maze that they have to walk. If it is inside, masking tape will do the trick. Their goal is to walk the entire line, heel to toe, without falling into the imaginary burning lava that is glowing on either side of the line. Their focus is on their task and not the chaotic thoughts consuming them.

Guided Imagery

Have your child get into a comfortable position. Then, have them think of somewhere they would like to be. They should picture that place in their mind. Then, they should use their senses to explore that place in their mind. For example, if they want to go camping, then they can use their senses to smell the campfire. They can see the marshmallows turn brown as they roast them, and then taste the sweetness as they eat them. They can hear the insects and birds talking, along with the sounds of the squirrels and rabbits scurrying through the woods.

Another way to practice guided imagery is to have your child lay down and pretend they are laying near a river. They can picture themselves putting their negative thoughts and feelings into the water and watching them float away. Then, they can pull positive thoughts out of the water and put them into their head.

If they are a Harry Potter fan, they can picture themselves putting their thoughts into Professor Dumbledore's pensieve, the cauldron that holds all of the wizard's thoughts. This idea can be substituted with other similar concepts that you and/or your child may be interested in.

More on Guided Imagery

Have them relax. Then, they should think of a small ball of light in their favorite color. This is a relaxation ball that will allow them to focus. The ball should start at their toes and work their way up to their head. As the ball moves, it will absorb all of their extra energy, allowing their body to

relax. When it gets to their head, it will take out all of the chaotic and negative thoughts and feelings, leaving only the positive ones behind.

They should concentrate on the ball taking away the negative and
leaving only the positive while feeling their body physically relaxing. This
can be a great way to help them sleep.

Cloud Meditation

Have you ever watched the clouds and tried to find shapes in them?
Watching clouds is a great meditation technique for your child. They can
sit or stand, whichever they prefer. Then, they can attach a frustrating
thought or feeling to a cloud and watch it float away in the sky. As a new
cloud appears, they can take a positive thought or feeling and send up
another negative one.

They can also count how long it takes for a cloud to move past a specific
point.

Progressive Muscle Relaxation

This is a great meditation technique, especially if your child is feeling
anxious or worried about something, or if your child has been finding it
difficult to sleep (which can be an issue for kids with ADHD).

With this technique, your child would find someplace comfortable to
relax. Then, starting at the very tip of their toes, they would clench them as
tight as they can, and then completely relax them. They would move their
feet, calves, all the way up their body. Many times, this technique will put
them to sleep.

Stuffed Animal

Everyone has that favorite stuffed animal they loved to play with as a
kid. Have your child pick out one of their favorite toys and put it on their
belly. They should lay down on the floor or somewhere else. Then, they
should watch the toy rise and fall with their breath, making sure they don't
knock it off their belly. Their entire focus should be on the stuffed toy as
they rock it to sleep.

Walking Meditation

This is a great way to help your child meditate because they can move at the same time. As you walk, tell them to pay close attention to how it feels as they take a step. Tell them to pay attention to the sound it makes. Ask them to think about how it feels as their knee bends with each stop. This will help them make a connection to their body and mind, while at the same time, calming their thoughts. Exercising also increases dopamine levels, which is an added bonus to this meditation technique.

Freeze Game

Have your child walk, hop, or dance. Then, when you say freeze, they have to stay perfectly still. Ask them to consider what it feels like to stay frozen. They should notice how it feels to stay perfectly still as opposed to moving and dancing around.

Mindfulness

Mindfulness and meditation often go hand in hand. Meditation is often used to help you focus your mind for a time or thinking deeply about a particular subject. The goal is to train your mind to increase your attention and awareness. It is designed to help you find calm.

The goal of mindfulness is to be present in the moment by focusing on thoughts and sensations around you without casting any judgment. It is about paying full attention to what is happening in your mind and around you.

Mindful Coloring

Have your child choose a crayon, pen, pencil, marker, etc. to color or draw with. As they are coloring, have them focus on the sounds of the media as it moves across the paper. Ask them to think about how it feels moving the instrument across the paper. The purpose is to get them to focus on the sounds and sensations as they color or draw, which then calms the boomeranging thoughts bouncing in their head.

STOP

The STOP technique can be beneficial for children who can determine when they are feeling frustrated, upset, or just overwhelmed by the thoughts that are constantly swimming around in their heads.

The S stands for stop anytime they are feeling upset or stressed out. This is a good time for them to take a step back from the situation that could be causing them stress, even if it is a mental step back.

Taking a couple of breaths or engaging in the breathing exercises is the T part of this technique. Using the four square or three triangle technique can help their body and mind start to calm down.

The O represents observe. Your child in this part should then observe what is around them . Even if they are in a boring place, such as a classroom, there is something they can focus on, such as a pattern on the floor or a mark on the wall. They can focus on the noises that are going on around him, even if it is the sound of their heart beating or their breathing.

Proceeding is the P. Once the anxiety or stress has gone away, your child can then proceed with the rest of their day.

Have a SEAT

This technique works well with older kids, although some younger children could benefit from this technique, as well. Have your child sit down somewhere comfortable. Then, they should think about the sensations they are feeling. Is the air cool or warm? What do they smell? What sounds do they hear?

The E stands for emotions. What are they feeling? Are they sad, happy, or just indifferent?

Considering what actions they want to take is the next part of this technique. What do they want to do?

The last part of this is your child asking themselves what thoughts have come into their head. What are they thinking?

This technique can help your child figure out what they are thinking and feeling, as well as what is causing these emotions.

"I Notice."

This is a variant of the game, "I spy." This game is designed to help your child become more aware of what is around him and may pick up on items they never noticed before. You can ask them to find an object with a rough texture. They might see the tree in the yard, a fence post, or any number of other objects.

Happiness Journal

A happiness journal is a great tool to help your child focus on the positive things that have occurred during the day. At the end of every night, they should write three good things that happened during the day. Even if the day was rough, they will learn that there are always good things if they look for them.

Glitter Jars

A glitter jar is a great way to practice mindfulness. Fill a jar three quarters of the way up with water and put in a couple of spoons of glitter. Then, your child can shake the jar. The glitter floating around, without any form or structure, represents how they feel when they are upset and angry. Then, when the glitter settles on the bottom, their emotions are under control. Watching the glitter float around and then settle actually be quite calming.

Yoga

Yoga brings up images of people in stretch pants trying to achieve impossible positions. However, like meditation, these images are not what the practice is all about. There are many different forms of yoga that your child can engage in that will help them control symptoms associated with ADHD.

However, there is one stereotype associated with yoga that really is beneficial. It is the *"om"* sound. When you make the sound, it vibrates the vagus nerve. When the nerve vibrates, it reduces your heart rate and helps calm your nervous system.

There are many yoga positions your child can achieve that will help them calm their thoughts and feelings. Yoga encourages your child to focus on what pose they are trying to achieve and maintain. They are learning control. Your child with this technique can learn to focus on their actions and thoughts to contain their impulsiveness.

One study found that after eight weeks of practicing yoga, children who suffer from ADHD increased their ability to pay attention and focus on tasks, as well as their impulse control. According to the study, the children participated twice per week for 40 minutes. These children increased their accuracy and response times on two separate cognitive tests.

The breathing component that accompanies yoga can help your child feel as though they have more control over their mind and body.

It is great practice to work out with your child. Not only is yoga beneficial for you, but it can also help create a way to connect with your child and motivate them to do the yoga moves.

Control

Your child can practice control by using breathing exercises. Although several breathing exercises will be discussed a little bit later in the chapter, one in particular was recommended by Stacy Turis, who writes for ADDitude, a website/magazine dedicated to ADD and ADHD. It is the five-five-five method. Your child would breathe in through their nose, slowly, to the count of five. Then, they will hold their breath for the count of five, and then release their breath through their mouth to the count of five.

Concentration, Attention Span, and Focus

When your child is concentrating on their breathing or how their arms and legs feel while they are stretching them, they are learning to be aware of their body. It helps them focus their attention on their actions, which means their attention is in one place instead of bouncing off of the walls. The great news is that the self control they will learn while practicing yoga will be used in the classroom and at home.

Mountain Pose is the pose recommended for concentration by Turis.

> "Stand up straight with feet together. Spread the toes and straighten the legs without locking the knees. Ground down by pushing through the feet and lift the head, making sure to face forward, keeping your head level. Hold for ten deep breaths."

Confidence

Yoga can help your child gain confidence because they will be trying new poses and learning new skills. Learning how to control their emotions and actions, as well as how to calm themselves, will help them become more confident when interacting with their peers.

There are many children who would rather not try anything new in order to avoid the risk of failure. However, yoga allows them to try new poses. They will not always be successful and will sometimes end up falling; however, this is something they can laugh about and try again.

Turis recommends the roaring lion pose to help your child build confidence. She stated that this is a favorite with kids because they get to make funny faces and roar like they are the supreme ruler of the jungle.

> "Kneeling on the floor with their bottom resting on their calves, have them place their hands on the knees and sit up straight. Open the mouth, close the eyes, wrinkle the nose, and extend the tongue as far out and down as possible. Inhale and breathe out with a forceful ROARRRRR. Repeat five times."

Yoga Instills Calmness

Yoga can help your child be calm. This is especially true after they have practiced the same yoga poses and become good at them. Getting on the yoga mat or just the floor means they are ready to focus on their body and mind as they concentrate on getting into the poses and holding them, as well as practicing their breathing.

They should always start with deep breathing exercises. Then, they can find eight or ten poses to start practicing. Then, once they become an expert at those initial poses, they can find a couple more to add to their practice. They should keep the poses they practice in the same order because that will help with consistency.

One pose that Turis said your child can start with is the child's pose.

> "Kneeling on the floor with their bottom resting on their calves, have them place their hands on the knees and sit up straight. Open the mouth, close the eyes, wrinkle the nose, and extend the tongue as far out and down as possible. Inhale and breathe out with a forceful ROARRRRR. Repeat five times."

Other Calming Activities

Besides meditation, yoga, and mindfulness, there are several other activities that your child can engage in that will help them improve their focus and calmness while decreasing impulsivity.

Knitting

Knitting is a very calming activity. It helps improve your child's concentration, coordination, and control. The added bonus is that it can also teach a bit of math, since there is a lot of counting involved. The yarn and feel of the knitting needles also increase sensory feeling. The texture of the yarn, smoothness of the needles, and sound of them clicking together tantalize the senses. If knitting is too much of a challenge, then crocheting or finger knitting could be an option.

Regardless of how they choose to work, the repetition of the movements is very calming. The best part is that they will feel proud of themselves after they create something.

Gardening

Research has found that being close to nature can help improve symptoms of ADHD. Digging in the dirt is a great way to calm a hyperactive child. It is repetitive, so there is the calming effect. The feel of the tool and dirt, sounds that are part of the outdoors, and smells all engage their senses. They can dig up weeds from the yard or plant a flower or vegetable garden. The best part is that this activity is productive, and they can get a sense of accomplishing a goal.

There are other reasons why gardening can help your child. For one, taking care of a garden can teach them about responsibility and taking care of another living thing. Gardening also helps them establish a routine, such as watering the garden every day after school and pulling weeds on Saturday morning.

Another added bonus of gardening is that it can create an opportunity for your child to develop social skills if they with their siblings or in a community garden.

If you don't have the land or space for a regular garden, then you can have them cultivate container gardens.

. . .

Coloring

Coloring is a great way for your child to calm down and focus. Like with meditation practices, they can focus on the sounds of the crayon, smell of the wax, and how it feels as they rub the color off on the paper. Drawing can also allow your child to express what is bothering them without having to try to find the right words. Many times, bad behavior is simply an act of frustration because they know of no other way of telling someone that they are stressed, hurt, or feeling anxious.

Coloring—and other activities similar to this—can help the amygdala, the fear center in the brain, relax.

Weighted Blankets

Weighted blankets have been proven to calm people down. The weight of the blanket simulates deep pressure stimulation, which is a therapeutic technique. This technique uses pressure to relax the nervous system, thus helping to relieve pain, decrease anxiety, and improve your child's mood.

Nature Sounds

The sounds of a thunderstorm and rain or wolves howling can be soothing to some people. Others might find the sounds of a flute, violin, or waterfalls soothing. YouTube has a lot of audio recordings of these types of sounds. Playing some of these and asking your child to pay attention to the tempo of the rain or rhythm of the waterfall can help soothe them and calm their anxiety.

Taking a Walk

Your child is hyperactive. Sometimes, just taking a walk around the block or along the woods will help them find the words to express how they are feeling and what might be frustrating or agitating them. Once they express how they are feeling, it can help them calm down. Then, you can work with your child to help them find a solution to their problems.

5-4-3-2-1 Grounding Technique

This grounding technique can help your child focus their mind and find a sense of calm. It focuses on using their five senses. Although this technique can help them release anxiety and any frustrations, your child may perceive it as a game. You would ask your child to name five things that they can see, four things they can hear, three things they can feel, two things they can smell, and one thing they can taste.

Mastery

Everyone feels more successful if they can accomplish something or master a task. It provides a sense of accomplishment. It increases self-confidence and self-esteem. You can devise a task that your child can easily and successfully complete. You can also find something new for them to learn. Once they have learned that new skill, talent, concept, etc., then it is time to celebrate. Let them know that you are proud of them.

Breathing Exercises

Everyone breathes, and many of the techniques used in meditation, yoga, mindfulness, etc., focus on breathing. That is because breathing helps you control your thoughts and emotions. The idea isn't that your child *is* breathing (although that is still very important). It is *how* they are breathing. Most people take shallow breaths. However, when you practice taking deeper breaths, the extra oxygen will increase your sense of well-being and energy levels, and not the hyperactive type. It helps decrease anxiety and grumpiness.

Breathing through their diaphragm is very important because it will help them focus and control their impulsive behavior. Studies have shown that breathing using one's diaphragm activates the parasympathetic nervous system (PNS). The PNS regulates the body's stress levels, among other things. For example, if you jump out of a closet and scare your child, then it will be the PNS that calms their thundering heart.

Breathing Apps

Would you believe there are apps for these? They vary in price. The free apps are listed here, although it would be easy to find the paid apps by searching on any search engine or in any app store.

One app is Breathe, Think, Do Sesame. For this app, one of the monsters is dealing with a frustrating situation. Your child can help the monster by learning how to take deep breaths. There are YouTube versions as well. This app is free.

Super Stretch Yoga teaches 12 different yoga poses, along with how to calm down and practice breathing exercises. This app is designed for preschool and elementary-aged children.

There are other apps that might be able to help your child that you would have to pay for, such as Headspace for kids, Stop, Breathe, and Think Kids.

One negative aspect of these apps that you would need to think about is that the blue light emitted from the phones could cause your child to have problems sleeping.

The 7/11 Breath

This is not about running to the local convenience store and buying some chocolate, although sometimes a bag of M&Ms sounds like it would be a perfect solution.

The 7/11 breath is actually used by many people who find themselves in stressful situations, such as the police, athletes, and even teachers with a class of thirty kids, at least a quarter of whom have ADHD. According to psychiatrist Christopher Willard, even LeBron James uses this technique.

For this method, your child would breathe in for seven seconds, and then breathe out for 11 seconds. All the thoughts playing ping pong inside your child's head should quiet after they have done this a couple of times. It may even help them feel calmer physically. After 12 to 15 repetitions of the 7/11 breath, your child will be breathing between four and six breaths per minute. According to Dr. Willard, research has found that breathing at four to six breaths per minute can help strengthen long-term focus.

4-7-8 Breathing

This method of breathing was created by Dr. Andrew Weil. For this method, your child would breathe in through their nose for four seconds, hold it for seven, and then breathe out through their nose for eight. The purpose for this breathing method is the same as the other techniques. First, focusing on their breathing helps them concentrate on one concept instead of other thoughts and feelings floating around. Second, it calms them physically.

By breathing in deeply, they are increasing the amount of oxygen that goes to their brain and rest of the body, which in turn increases the amount of blood flow through. This will help them think more clearly.

Create a Breath Button

As you know, breathing is one of the most important aspects of meditation. It can help your child understand that it feels good to take a deep breath and let it go. As they let their breath go, they can focus on letting go of their stress, anxiety, or other negative or disruptive feelings.

The breath button is a great way to encourage them to use the breathing technique. The button can be a doorknob, light switch, or even a picture drawn on a piece of paper. Each time they touch the button, they would take in a deep breath through their nose, then let it out through their mouth.

This practice will encourage them to stop and think about what they are thinking and feeling. Because these breaths are calming, it can help them instill calm into their every day routine. The best aspect about this practice is that it can help them calm their thoughts and anxiety as they leave the house to go to school or visit a friend, especially if the doorknob is their breath button. The last act they would do before they leave the house is take that calming, cleansing breath.

LED Lights

LED lights that change colors are another tool that can be used to help your child meditate. Set the light on a table in front of them. They should breathe in when the light changes, and then breathe out as the light changes again. This will allow them to focus on the act of breathing instead of the rambling thoughts that bounce around in their brain.

Hot Chocolate Breath

Have your child pretend that they are holding a cup of hot chocolate in their hands next to their face. Then, have them breathe in deeply as though they are smelling the scent of the chocolate. Have him breathe out through their mouth as though they are cooling the chocolate off before they take a drink. Not only does this help them focus on their breathing, but when they get agitated, you can tell them to practice the chocolate breath to calm down.

Square Breathing

Square breathing focuses on using one's diaphragm to breathe. For this exercise, your child would take a deep breath in for four seconds and watch their belly rise. They should hold this breath for four seconds, and then breathe out for four seconds. Then, they would wait for four seconds before repeating this routine. They can put their hands on their stomach to watch the rise and fall with their breath.

Triangle Breathing

Triangle breathing is the same as square breathing except for two things. The first is that the breathing takes place to the count of three. So, your child would breathe in to a count of three, hold it for a count of three, and then breathe out to a count of three. The second difference is that there is no time between repetitions. Instead, they would simply breathe in again after the breath is released.

Back to Back Breathing

Back to back breathing is one method that might actually get your child to sit down for a couple of minutes. This meditation method is one that you can do with your child, or better yet, get one of their siblings to work with them, if they have any. That way, you can get more of your children involved.

Have your kids find a comfortable place where they can sit back to back. Their goal is to control their breathing so they are breathing in and out in sync. They will be so focused on their breathing that the rest of the chaos in their minds will be quieted. It will help them make a connection between their minds, emotions, and bodies.

Support Groups

Support groups for your child can be a great way to help them learn to cope with the symptoms that arise from ADHD. First, they can meet other children who have ADHD as well. They can learn how others handle the stress and frustrations. They can also learn tips on how to be successful in school and at home. Most importantly, they can form bonds with other people with the same problems and issues as they do, and who will not judge them for those issues.

AFTERWORD

Medication and therapy with counselors, therapists, psychologists, and other specialists are an important part of helping your child with ADHD be successful. However, there are many ways that you, as their parent, can also help them be successful. These methods don't cost you anything other than your time.

The benefits of these methods are numerous. First, they can help your child learn to focus and concentrate better. They help them curb their impulsiveness and take control of their mind and body. They help them find physical and mental calm in a chaotic world.

Most importantly, they provide a great way for you to connect with your child.

Chapter Summary

- Although medication and therapy are important to help your child cope with the symptoms of their ADHD, there are other methods as well.
- Meditation, yoga, breathing exercises, and mindfulness have all been proven to help children who suffer from ADHD.
- You can participate in these activities as well, giving you a great opportunity to connect with your child.

In the next chapter, you will learn parenting tips and techniques for a child with ADHD.

4
_____

CHAPTER FOUR: PARENTING TIPS

*L*eave it to Beaver, *The Cosby Show,* and *Family Ties* all show the perfect family. Yet, just like some people complain that fairy tales make young girls expect every man to be like Prince Charming, these television shows distort the reality of what real families look like.

Children do not come with their own "how-to" manuals. If they did, parenting would be a breeze. People learn to be parents from their own parents, television shows, books on the subject, and even classes. However, sometimes, you have a child that doesn't respond to anything that you have studied so far.

The fact is that even if you have a dozen children, they are all going to be different in how they act, think, and feel. Identical twins don't even think and act the same. This is especially true if you have a child who suffers from ADHD. If you have more than one child with ADHD,—which is entirely possible since it tends to run in families—then you might find yourself at a loss.

Raising children without ADHD can be hard enough. However, if your child has this disorder, then their brain functions completely differently than their peers. Even though they can learn the difference between appropriate and inappropriate behaviors, they are still more apt to act impulsively.

Taking parenting skills is not a bad thing, and doesn't mean you're a bad parent. It simply means that your kid has extra needs that you may need to accommodate, and you could possibly use some pointers.

Parenting classes can help you learn tools to understand and handle your child's behavior better. There are several techniques you might learn in a parenting skills class.

Understand

Understand what, you might ask. The fact is that there are a lot of aspects about your child that you have to understand.

One is that when they say and do hurtful things, it is not necessarily your child who is saying and doing these things; it is the mental disorder that is talking and acting. Many of these actions will decrease with age and if you have them practice the techniques discussed in the last chapter.

Another thing that you have to understand is that they are not likely being willfully disobedient. They might not be listening to you because they really and truly don't hear you. Their mind is going a million miles an hour, and they might know that you spoke, but the words aren't registering for them.

Because of their inability to control their actions, they might embarrass you by saying or doing things at just the wrong time. There is also nothing like that embarrassing temper tantrum right in the middle of the grocery store when everybody in town is out shopping at the same store.

It is also important to understand that your child's ADHD symptoms impact the entire family. Your child may lose things, get distracted easily, or have other issues that keep the entire family waiting. Their symptoms may cause problems with their siblings that they just don't understand. Unfortunately, these can cause additional stress and frustration for you.

In addition, it is extremely important to understand that you have to take care of yourself mentally and physically. You can't take care of anyone else unless you are okay. When you get on an airplane, one of the instructions given to passengers is that you need to put on your own oxygen mask before you can help your children or anyone else. If you can't breathe, you won't be able to help your family breathe either.

Reward System and Discipline

One is to use immediate rewards for positive behavior. Long-term rewards are not as effective, since kids with ADHD struggle with waiting.

Chores should be broken down into smaller tasks. For example, if you want your child to pick up the toys in their room, maybe they can pick up everything that is blue first. That will keep the task from becoming too overwhelming and might turn it into a game, making it fun. If there are weekly chores that they need to get done, then you can create a list and color code or organize them in such a way that they know exactly what they need to accomplish without getting overwhelmed.

Giving timeouts is not just about disciplining your child. Sometimes simply extracting them from the stressful situation can help them calm down. It can teach them that, in the future, when they find themselves in a stressful or overwhelming situation, to walk away for a few minutes and cool down. Explain to your child ahead of time that timeouts are for thinking about their behavior and considering how they should have handled the situation better.

If they have a meltdown in public, you should take them away from the situation as soon as possible. You should stay calm and purposeful while removing them from the area.

As hard as it may be, it is essential that you stay calm during these situations. If you are upset and agitated yourself, it will only make your child more upset. However, if you are calm, it will be a lot easier to help your child calm down.

Instead of rewarding your child with food or toys, use praise, privileges, or activities. You should change the reward occasionally because your child will get bored if the reward is always the same. Ask them what they would like as a reward. If it is reasonable, then make it a deal. It is important that you always follow through with the reward.

Consequences should always be known in advance. Then, when a misdeed occurs, you should follow through with the consequence immediately. It is important that you always follow through on a consequence. If a certain behavior is only disciplined once in a while, then your child will be confused as to whether it is acceptable and with what they can get away with.

When your child does misbehave, ask them to reflect on the situation. They should think about what happened and what their reaction to the trigger was. Then, they should think about why it was wrong and what they could have done better in the future.

It is important that you and your partner are in agreement with how to reward and discipline your child. First, the arguments that would occur between the two of you could cause more harm to your child's emotional state. Second, when rewards and discipline are not administered consistently, your child may become confused, as they will not understand what is expected of them.

Connect with Your Child

Another technique you can use to get a better understanding of your child is through scheduling specific time to be together. By playing or working on projects together, you can see how your child tackles those problems and handles stressful situations. It will also give you the opportunity to see, and praise them, for their strengths and abilities.

Understand that your child might have some personality traits that you think are peculiar. As long as they aren't harmful to themselves or anyone else, then accept them as a part of who they are. It is harmful to try to change your child's personality traits just because they are different from other people's. That is part of what makes your child unique and wonderful.

Flexibility

It is important to be flexible. If you see that your child really is trying to make a difference, and the phone calls from their teacher had been reduced from three a week to once a week, then you can still give them the reward, even if the goal was zero calls.

Another way to be flexible is to compromise with your child. If they did two out of the three chores you asked them to do, and it seems like getting that third chore completely done might be an issue, then still praise them for a good job and either help them with the third or let it slide, at least until later. The positivity will go a long way in helping them grow.

Give your child credit for what they have done and accept it. If you are a perfectionist and expect them to get 100 percent of their chores done, then you are setting them up for failure. Neither of you will be satisfied. This will not only damage their self-esteem, but it could also harm your relationship with them.

Structure

Structure is a very important part of helping your child be successful. For example, to keep them from becoming overwhelmed with too much stimulation, you might limit their playdates to just one or two friends.

Providing structure, even during play time, can help your child deal with their ADHD. Hyperactivity can climb to high levels if they are left on their own without structure. Specific rituals during meals, homework times, and bedtime can make these events go a lot smoother for both of you.

Clocks and Timers

These items can be very valuable when you are trying to get your child through their day. One clock should be in their bedroom so they know what time they should get up at, get dressed, finish with their chores, etc. A timer will let them know when it is time to put their toys away and get ready for bed. Clocks and timers are essential tools for providing structure for your child while they are at home.

Make Their Schedule Simple

Keeping track of a busy schedule is extremely difficult. You have to remember where everyone needs to be, at what time they have to be there, and when they are finished. For a child with ADHD whose mind and life is already filled with chaos, this can be overwhelming. Mondays and Wednesdays are ball practice, Tuesdays are Scouts, Thursdays are violin, and Friday nights are Tae Kwon Do. This schedule can be enough to make anyone feel overwhelmed.

Keeping them busy in an effort to help control their hyperactivity is not a good solution. Instead, a busy schedule would make them even more distracted. Limit their afterschool activities to just a few based on their interests and abilities.

Keep Them Busy

Wait a minute. I just said you should keep their schedule simple. Now I'm saying you should keep them busy?

There is a fine line between keeping your child busy and not overwhelming them with so many activities that they don't know what is going on.

When you organize your child's calendar, set up a specific time for them to practice their breathing techniques or mindful coloring. Put in a slot for helping you cook or make cookies. These activities will give them something to focus on without overwhelming them.

It is important to avoid television and video games as much as possible. First, technology gives access to so much information at once, which can be overwhelming. Second, constant action can actually rev up your child's hyperactivity. Third, the blue light can disrupt their circadian rhythms, or natural body rhythms, which could disrupt their sleep patterns. Fourth, a lot of the television shows or video games, even the ones that are supposed to be made for kids, can potentially be violent. The violence can exacerbate the symptoms of your child's ADHD.

Quiet Place

Create a quiet place for your child where they can go if they are starting to feel overwhelmed or stressed out. Even adults need some time to just get away from the chaos that is our lives. A beanbag chair in a corner away from the television, rest of the family, and other potential distractions can help your child learn to manage their behavior. They can have a book nearby, some coloring supplies, or other items that can calm and help them regain control of their emotions.

The quiet place should *not* be the same place that you send them for a timeout.

Try to Stay Neat and Organized

This is easy to say, but far harder to accomplish. You have a child who will start drawing, get distracted, and leave their stuff out. While you are trying to get them to pick up after themselves, you have another child who suddenly decides that the middle of the living room is the best place for their pants. Your world is crazy, and keeping everything put up neatly and organized seems like a feat better suited for Hercules.

However, it is important that you *do* keep your home neat and organized, so your child with ADHD understands that everything has its place. When an item is not being used, it should be put back in that rightful place. Enlist the help of your children. This will set a good example for your child and help them understand that even their items have a specific place to go, and they should be neat and organized.

Color Coordinate

One of the struggles your child might face due to their ADHD is being unorganized and unable to find what they need. However, there are ways to handle this situation. In addition to having a specific place where everything goes, you might think about color coding bins or crates. For example, their school supplies and homework go in the blue container, and their arts and crafts items go in the red container. Not only will this help them find their things easily, but it will also help them put their things away.

Color coding a calendar can also be a huge help. Children with ADHD need help with organization and structure. A calendar with a list of activities, chores, etc., is a great way to help them with these struggles by helping them understand it better. For example, morning routines might be written in green ink, whereas any school activities would be written in red ink. That way, they can see at a glance what is expected of them at that specific time.

While you are at it, you can color code their behavior chart. School behaviors, such as raising their hand before speaking or staying in their seat, can be written in red, whereas their chores can be written in blue. Other desired behaviors, such as sharing his toys with their younger siblings, can be in a different color.

Limit Technology

Children who suffer from ADHD are easily drawn to accessible distractions. Technology, such as television and video games, can encourage impulsive behavior because everything is constantly moving and changing. Instead, increase play time outside. Not only will a nice game of tag or basketball help them focus their attention on one task, but they will also be able to release some of that excessive energy.

Exercise

Along the same lines, you should encourage your child to exercise and take part in sports and other events. Exercise can help them focus on the movements of their body. For example, people who run track have a specific form that they use to increase speed and durability. Martial artists have poses and specific movements that they use. The link between the body and mind are reinforced.

In addition, exercise helps improve concentration and decrease impulsive behaviors. Exercise decreases the risk of depression and anxiety by increasing dopamine levels. Dopamine is a chemical created and released by the brain. It is also known as one of the feel-good chemicals.

There are several professional athletes who say they suffer from ADHD. Getting involved in some type of sport, whether it is martial arts, swimming, team sports, or whatever they enjoy helped them. Similarly, it can allow your child to engage in and focus on something they are passionate about. It is also a great way to get rid of excess energy.

Sleep Is Important

Just as it is extremely important that your child has time to be active and release their energy, it is equally important that they get adequate rest. Establish a specific bedtime and time to get up in the mornings. Doing so will let their body get the proper sleeping rhythm, which in turn means they will get better rest. A lack of rest can make their ADHD symptoms even worse. Fatigue can make it harder to pay attention and focus on tasks. It also decreases their ability to control their impulses. To this end, you should limit or eliminate sugar and caffeine, especially several hours before bed. You should also decrease their television time and other electronics for at least an hour before bed because the lights can keep them awake.

Instead, establish a calm bedtime ritual. First, they would take a bath or shower, which is soothing. Then, they can brush their teeth. Afterwards, they can read or color for half an hour or an hour before bedtime. These are calm activities. Once this pattern is established, their brain will recognize that when they take a shower, it is time to slow down and get into resting mode.

Encourage Them to Think and Wait

Impulsiveness is an issue that many kids with ADHD struggle with. They will blurt out what they are thinking or act without any forethought. One way you can help your child is to encourage them to think out loud before they take any action. They can state out loud what they want to do and the reasons why they might want to take those actions.

This works for a couple of reasons. First, it makes them pause to think about what is happening and the potential consequences of their actions. Second, when you hear something out loud, it triggers a different part of your brain, and you process the information differently than when you simply think about it.

An added bonus to this technique is that you can hear your child's thought processes and have a better understanding of them. You can then be in a better position to help them curb their impulses.

By the same token, you can help your child learn to think before speaking impulsively. This will not only help them stay out of trouble in school or avoid saying something they might regret, but it can also teach them to give more thoughtful answers. For example, you might ask them which is his favorite Avenger and why. Then, tell them they can't answer for at least thirty seconds because they have to think about it.

Plan Ahead

Oftentimes, even the youngest child knows what frustrates them and makes them angry. It could be when their sibling touches their stuff or when a certain person at school looks at them weird. Talk to your child and let them know that in life, frustrating things will happen, and they can't control other people's actions. What they *can* do, however, is control how they react to them. Help them plan a strategy that allows them to react positively to the issue. They can tell mom that their sibling is doing it again and simply ignore the person giving them funny looks. It could be something that you would practice with them.

Be Positive

In 1988, Bobby McFerrin wrote a song called *Don't Worry, Be Happy*. Two lines are "In every life we have some trouble, but when you worry you make it double." It sounds simple, but it does have a ring of truth to it. There are going to be stressful days with your child. It is important to stay positive. Praise and celebrate the good behavior and times.

When there is bad behavior and stressful times, remember that tomorrow is a new day. Tomorrow, you get to try again with a clean slate. Try not to get upset or negative. Just take everything one day at a time, or even hour by hour if you have to.

. . .

Keep Your Sense of Humor

It seems that all children find a way to embarrass their parents one way or another, regardless of whether they suffer from ADHD. However, because your child does suffer from ADHD, they will have trouble controlling their impulses. This means they will often speak and act before they think about it. They have a tendency to repeat exactly what you said, out of context, just at the wrong time, or report on something you did in the most embarrassing manner. It could be very embarrassing today, but later on, it will give you something to laugh about.

For example, as a therapist, I was working with a woman who had a child with ADHD. The woman's husband would sometimes walk by and playfully pat her butt. One day, in the middle of a church service, her son announced in a loud voice, "Daddy spanks my mommy."

They laugh now, but she was mortified at the time.

Be Calm

It is important that you maintain your calm. If you are agitated and loud, then the issue will only escalate. However, if you are able to stay calm, it will be easier for your child to be calm. If you feel as though steam is about to erupt from your ears, and your head is going to pop off, walk away for a minute. Use mindful breathing techniques or take a walk. Then, when you feel as though you can be calm with your child, then you can address the situation.

Believe in Your Child

I once attended a meeting where the parents were asked to name some positive things about their child. None of them could come up with a single good thing. It wasn't because the child was that bad; it was because they were unable to cope with the negative aspects of their child's disability.

Make a list of all the great things about your child that you love. Think about all the goofy things they do, their sense of humor, and what makes them unique. Revisit this list often, not just when you are upset.

Believe that, although they might have some challenges to deal with now, they will be successful in life. They will learn, grow, and mature.

Maintain Control

Sometimes, life with a child who suffers from ADHD can be a struggle. they don't want to follow rules, and their behavior and attitude are getting to be downright ugly. However, you are the parent, and it is essential that you maintain control in your home and make sure they follow the rules. Be patient with them and nurture them. However, don't allow them and their behavior to intimidate or bully you.

Don't Blame Others

It is easy to cast blame on other people for your child's behavior. After all, it is in a parent's nature to protect their child. However, if your child is always getting in trouble at school, you can't say that it is the teacher's fault that they can't control their class, or that they don't know how to teach your child who suffers from a disability.

This would allow your child to have an easy way out. They wouldn't have to take responsibility for their own actions if someone else is always getting blamed for them.

Be a Team of Problem Solvers

"How many times have I told you to clean your room? What's wrong with you?" Although these words, said with frustration, are meant to encourage your child to clean their room, all it really does is hurt their self-esteem.

A better approach is to team up with your child. First, explain the issue and why it is a problem. Carol Brady, a child psychologist in Houston, Texas said, "Parents must make ADHD the enemy—not the child. When you personalize a child's ADHD associated problems, her self-esteem plummets. But when you team up with your child to problem solve various negative behaviors, you create a climate where your child feels loved and supported despite her shortcomings."

Therefore, instead of berating your child when their room still isn't clean in spite of how you asked them three times to clean it and even offered a reward if it was done, you should approach it as a team problem. Explain there is a problem, and you need your child's help to solve the problem. You can explain that you are afraid you will trip over the toys left in the middle of the floor, or that leaving food in their bedroom is going to invite bugs. Then, ask for your child's help in creating a solution.

. . .

Don't Make "No" Your Automatic Answer

There are many parents who say no simply out of reflex. Other times, parents feel as though they have a good reason for saying no, such as worrying that their child will not be safe walking to school by themselves. Sometimes the "no" comes from fear, or simply because you are so tired that you are struggling to get your own tasks done.

Hearing that "n" word too often can make your child feel rebellious and more likely to give in to their impulsive desires.

Therefore, before you say "no," consider the request. You can also tell your child that you and they should sit down and come up with a good solution to their request. It makes your child feel as though they have a voice and some semblance of control in their life. It also helps them develop their problem solving skills and see the situation from your perspective. The great thing is that you also get to see the situation through their eyes.

Anticipate Situations that Could be Potentially Explosive

Oftentimes, parents of children with ADHD react to situations. Instead, you should think about activities that could cause your child to have a meltdown. Then, you can plan ahead how you will handle that situation if and when it occurs.

Before your child heads out to their friend's house or the mall, talk to them about what is expected from them and how they should act. You can also talk about potential situations that might come up and how they should handle those situations.

If something does occur, then you can pull them aside for a conversation about how to deal with the situation. If you and they can't come up with a solution, then it is time to leave—even if you have to leave behind a huge basket full of groceries.

Manage Your Stress

As a parent trying to take care of yourself, the rest of your family, and your job, a child with a disorder of this nature can create an incredible amount of stress. You might think that unless you clone yourself, you will never be able to handle everything thrown your way.

You are dealing with your child's school, and sometimes multiple phone calls a week about their behavior. You might find yourself explaining their behavior to friends and family who don't understand. You might be unable to go out and have a nice dinner just to relax because finding a babysitter who can cope with your child's behavior is very difficult. Not to mention, the work you have to miss taking them to therapy, meetings at school, and other issues.

Dealing with the increased stress might make you less aware of the differences in your child's behavior. This might make it harder for you to be aware of the nuances, or gradations, of your child's behavior. This, in turn, can make it harder for you to work with your child and their therapist to implement different techniques designed to help your child.

It is important that you find ways to manage your own stress. Exercising, meditating, hobbies, and other activities can help you take care of yourself and keep you from becoming too overwhelmed.

If life does become extremely overwhelming, then you should consider counseling. Counseling doesn't mean you're weak. What it does mean is that you need to talk out loud to an unbiased person. Sometimes, just talking to someone can make a difference. It never hurts to get other people's thoughts and ideas on a situation.

Take breaks when you need to. Needing a break from your child doesn't mean you're a bad parent. It means that you are human. It is important to step away from a situation if you are feeling overwhelmed by the chaos.

Visit a friend, take a walk, call a family member, take a bubble bath, go to the gym, or even sit in a corner and read a book when you need a break. If you need to, schedule some time alone on the calendar. That way, your child will know that they can read a book or color while you are also relaxing. If you need a night out, then hire a babysitter. Taking breaks is important because you have to be healthy if you plan to be supportive for your child.

When you are aggravated, find a way to calm yourself before you react. Kids with ADHD are just like all other children in mimicking what they see. If you become agitated and react negatively, they will copy that behavior. However, if they see that when you are agitated, you take a moment to breathe and compose yourself before reacting, they will absorb that behavior as well.

Remember that, although you can't see it, your child struggles from a mental disorder. Their brain doesn't work quite the same as everyone else's.

They're doing the very best they can, and like the rest of us, they will have their good days and bad days.

Impact on the Family

Your child with ADHD clearly struggles. They not only have to struggle with the external issues that arise, but also with the internal ones. They might not understand why they behave the way they do, and their thought process could be very frustrating.

You, as their parent, also feels the stress of their disability as you cope with the outward manifestations of their actions.

However, it is important to realize that the entire family is often affected by your child as well. Their siblings, as well as the parents, feel stress too. This stress can cause the family to be dysfunctional as a whole. It may also cause other family members to have internal and external problems.

Because of the amount of time and energy it takes to care for a child who suffers from ADHD, other siblings and perhaps even your partner may feel as though you don't have enough time for them. In addition, if their behavior impacts them in other ways, such as embarrassing them in front of their friends, lashing out, etc., there could be resentment felt toward your child.

Research has indicated that having a child with ADHD can have direct negative results on the parents. For example, parents of children with this disorder tend to consume more alcohol. Marital problems also seem to increase. Parents are more socially isolated from friends and family and have problems adjusting to the stress both emotionally and psychologically.

Education Programs

To counteract the stress and dysfunction caused by your child's disability, your family can become involved in an education program that can help all the family members understand what ADHD is and its effects. As a parent, you can learn that you are not responsible for your child's disability and learn techniques to help them become successful academically, socially, and personally. You will also be relieved to learn that as your child grows older and matures, many of the symptoms may not be quite as excessive.

Their siblings can learn what situations might make the symptoms worse or better. They will learn techniques to help them have a better relationship with them.

Social Support Systems

One type of a social support system is joining a group to connect with other parents who have children suffering from ADHD. This helps you know that you are not alone. It will help you find a way to relieve your stress and share your stressors and issues with people who completely understand where you are coming from. They can help you find ways to reduce your stress. In addition, you might also find someone who can care for your child for a few hours, so you can get that much needed adult time to re-energize yourself.

Therapy and Training Programs

Many of the therapy methods that work for children with ADHD involve the parents. The parents learn how to set up limits for their children and have a system of consequences and rewards. These therapy techniques will not only help your child, but also help you gain a sense of control over your child's behavior. It can increase your self-confidence as a parent and make you feel more satisfied.

You might also think about finding a therapy practice for yourself. For example, cognitive behavior therapy can help you change the negative thoughts you have about yourself, your parenting skills, and other stressors you have in your life.

Family therapy, or family based intervention therapies, may also be beneficial. This type of therapy isn't just about parenting skills for children with ADHD; it focuses on helping the entire family work together to decrease the anxiety, depression, and other stresses caused by living with someone with ADHD. ADHD doesn't just affect the child with the disability or the parents who are trying to help the child be successful. It affects everyone in the household. Doctors James Johnson, Lindsay McAlister, and Steven Reader said, "The problem of ADHD is not just the child's —it belongs to the entire family! And, in different ways, all may need help in coping with this disorder."

AFTERWORD

Being a parent is not an easy job. You have on-the-job training provided by the very people you are supposed to be guiding. This stress is doubled when you have a child who suffers from ADHD. Just when you think you have everything figured out, something else comes along and has you second guessing yourself and everything you've been doing.

The fact is that children aren't born with a how-to manual. And even if you've had a dozen other children, what worked for one isn't necessarily going to work for the other. Again, this is doubled when you have a child who suffers from ADHD.

Although ADHD does cause your child to exhibit frustrating behaviors, you can still have a happy healthy relationship with them and watch them grow into an incredible adult who is calm, can control their actions, thoughts, and feelings, and can curb their impulsiveness. The reward is certainly worth it.

Chapter Summary

- Parenting is a hard enough job as it is. When your child has ADHD, it can be even more challenging.
- There are many tips and techniques that you can use to help your child be successful in life.
- It is very important that you take care of yourself first.

In the next chapter, you will learn techniques and forms of interventions that will help your child be successful in school.

CHAPTER FIVE: TECHNIQUES AND INTERVENTIONS FOR SCHOOL

The school principal has called for the third time this week. Your child who suffers from ADHD has been in another fight, refused to sit down for silent reading time, stood on their head on the lunch table or ... the possibilities are endless.

You end the phone call and look up to see your boss tapping their shoe on the floor. They have three little perfect robots—I mean, children—who never have any difficulties, so they can't understand why you are having so much trouble with your child. They are there to inform you that if you are late one more time or take off early to deal with your child's school issues, then you will no longer be employed.

Great. You need a job. You need to be there for your child. And most importantly, you need your child to do well in school so they can have a great future. How can you make that happen?

There are techniques and interventions you can use to help your child achieve academic success and help you keep your job.

At Home

Children who suffer from ADHD tend to struggle in school. However, there are several ways you can help them be more successful academically. The first place to start is at home.

. . .

Schedule

Creating a schedule and sticking with it is one way you can help your child become more successful. Have a specific time that they would wake up each morning, eat breakfast, go to school, do homework, and go to bed. Schedule specific times for playing, watching television, and other activities as well. If possible, let your child help you create the schedule, and when it is completed, post it where they can have access to it when they need to view it.

Color coding this schedule can help them keep track of their tasks. There should be a place on the schedule that they can check off each time they accomplish a task.

Organization

To help your child stay organized, have a designated spot for things they use every day. For example, lay out their clothes (or have them lay out their own clothes) in a certain spot. Have a specific spot for their backpack, lunch box, and anything they might need for school. This will keep them from becoming overwhelmed when they need to find these items while helping them remember where they are. They should also have a designated, clearly labeled spot for toys, books, and other items.

Make sure they carry an organizer or planner with them to school. They should write down what homework they have in each class and what materials they need to bring home in order to complete those assignments. If they forget to write down their assignments, you might consider asking their teacher to sign their planner each day. You can initial each assignment as they complete it. Not only will this help them make sure they complete all their tasks, but it will also give them a sense of accomplishment.

Creating a quiet place for your child can also be beneficial. You can put a desk in a nook in your house that limits distractions. The space should be organized with everything they need to complete their homework assignments. Organization not only helps them know where everything they need is, but also helps teach them organization skills.

Break Down Tasks

One issue that kids with ADHD struggle with is handling larger tasks that are complicated or have several steps. You and your child's teacher can help prevent them from becoming overwhelmed by breaking these tasks into smaller, bite-sized chunks. As they accomplish each step, they can check it off the list. This will not only keep them from shutting down during intimidating tasks, but it can also give them a sense of accomplishment as they mark off each step.

Positive Reinforcement

Use positive reinforcement to help your child keep a healthy self-esteem. Because ADHD often makes your child struggle with sitting down and getting work done, they will often receive negative feedback. If they only get negative feedback, then it could have a bad effect on their self-esteem.

Provide Breaks

Breaking up homework times can help your child do better and be more willing to complete assignments. Have them work hard for 15 minutes. Then, give them five minutes to walk around, stretch, do jumping jacks, or some other physical activity. Not only will the breaks and physical activity help them deal with their inability to sit still for very long, but exercising and moving around will also increase blood flow to the brain.

Fidgets

Allowing your child to fidget while working on a project or homework can help them concentrate. There are a lot of fidget toys out there—many of which don't make noise—that kids can use to help them focus.

Exercise Before Homework

Let your child get out their excess energy by having playtime before they have to sit down and work for a longer period of time. This could be especially useful if they have just come home from school, where the kids were supposed to sit and work quietly all day. Your child likely has a lot of built up energy that is ready to explode out of them. Letting them get that out before sitting down to do homework will be beneficial in helping them sit still and focus on the task.

. . .

Exercise Before School

It may mean that you have to get up a little earlier in the morning than you really wanted to, but it could be a big help for your child.

Wake them up an hour earlier than they would need to if they were simply heading off to school. They should use that time to meditate, practice yoga, or simply run laps around the house. Letting them burn off the extra energy first thing in the morning before they even head off to school might allow them to spend more time in their seat focusing on their work rather than running laps around the classroom.

Work with Their Teacher and the School

Your child's teacher has a room full of children, all with different learning styles, needs, and personalities. In addition, they will also likely have at least one child with ADHD. Your child's teacher will do their very best to help ensure that your child learns while they are in school and help them be successful. However, this success will be a lot easier if you are involved in the process.

Communication

You are your child's voice. As their advocate, it is essential that you talk to the administrators, their teacher, and perhaps the special education teacher about the disabilities your child has and what they will need in order to be successful.

It is also very important that you are willing to listen to this same group of people and take into consideration what they are communicating to you. They share the same goal as you do. They want your child to be successful in school.

Regardless of how the communication takes place—whether it is a virtual meeting, phone call, or in person—it is important that it is positive, productive, and constructive. It is important that regardless of the nature of the phone call that you are calm, even if it is another phone call about your child's behavior. Be specific about the nature of your communication. If it is another call about his behavior, talk about how you and the school can work together to help them. Stay positive. Working together, you, their teacher, and the other school personnel can help your child be academically successful.

. . .

Plan Ahead for Meetings

Schedule specific times to talk to your child's teacher, the counselor, principal, and special education teacher, as well as any other people who will be involved in their education. If possible, schedule a meeting before the school year begins. Explain what your child's needs are and work with the school to map out a plan to help them be successful. Then, once the school year begins, schedule monthly meetings with their teachers and other educators to figure out how your child is doing, what interventions are working, and which are not.

Follow Through with Planned Meetings

Although their teacher and the other educators have good intentions, they may not always remember to follow through with the meetings. The same might happen for you. You have work, other children, and a million other things that you have to take care of. You feel like you are being pulled in different directions. The meeting just might slip your mind. Set a reminder to make sure the meetings happen. If it is possible, arrange for the meetings to take place in your child's classroom, so you can see their learning environment. It will make it easier for you to come up with workable solutions as far as seating arrangements and other accommodations to help them focus.

Create Goals as a Team

Discuss your child's strengths and weaknesses. Share your determination that your child will achieve academic success. Then, work with the teachers to create goals and determine a plan of action to help your child reach their goals.

It is important that the goals are realistic. If your child is unable to sit still for the ten minutes of silent reading time, then the goal should be set at a point that they would be able to reach. Perhaps they can sit still for silent reading time for five minutes. Then, once they can reach that goal, then you can add an extra minute to it.

The other important aspect of the goal is that it should be measurable. They should be able to sit still during silent reading time for five minutes 80 percent of the time.

When they are able to meet that goal, then the team can meet again and adjust it.

. . .

Listen

Your child's teacher sees them every day. And like you, their goal is to help them be successful in school. It is important that you listen carefully to what your child's teacher has to say, even if it is hard to hear. The only way you can help your child succeed is if you understand their challenges so you can find solutions.

Share Your Information

To get a complete picture of your child, it is important that you share information about your child's history and past performances with their teachers. Talk about the medication that they are taking and the side effects of those drugs. You should also talk about any therapy they are involved in. By the same token, the teachers need to share their observations about their behaviors, abilities, and challenges. Your child will act differently when they are in school compared to how they will be at home. It is important that everyone involved has a full picture of your child.

Ask Hard Questions

Although the answers might be hard to hear, ask your child's teachers what problems they are having in the classroom and on the playground. This isn't just about behavior; it can be about learning problems as well. Many times, children with ADHD also have other learning disabilities. Ask the educators what services are available to help your child with their challenges.

At School

504 Plans

If necessary, you can work with your school to get a 504 plan, which provides your child with accommodations and modifications in the classroom to help complete assignments. A 504 plan describes the accommodations and modifications that are made within the classroom setting to help your child be more successful. The plan helps the teacher create a learning environment for your child to control their behavior and helps your child concentrate on their assigned tasks and have more academic success.

To qualify for a 504 plan, your child must have a diagnosis for a disability (ADHD does qualify) that restricts at least one or more significant life activities, such as having an inability to focus in class, being easily distracted, etc.

One of the hallmarks of ADHD is that your child is easily distracted. Any noise or movement that they catch out of the corner of their eye will capture their attention and change their focus from the task at hand to whatever else is going on. Sometimes, their mind will simply wander, and they might seem as though they are paying attention to the math lesson, but in reality, their brain is flying a spaceship.

Sitting then in the front of the classroom near the teacher can help them monitor your child's attention a little better—they can detect the glazed look that comes over their eyes when it occurs. The proximity to the teacher will also encourage your child to pay attention.

Being seated away from windows, doors, and friends will also help keep them from being distracted. They can be seated away from any of their classmates who might cause distractions.

Frequent breaks are another accommodation that your child might receive under the 504 plan. For example, state assessments are known to take a couple of hours. Your child could have a written accommodation that allows them to take breaks every half hour so they can stand up and stretch.

A 504 can provide your child with extra time to take important tests, quizzes, or complete important projects. This will keep them from making careless mistakes and feeling rushed.

Smaller settings for testing is another accommodation that your child can receive to possibly help them be more successful. They can test in a different classroom than their regular classroom, which can help them avoid being distracted from their peers. Also, there is less pressure to hurry up and finish tests.

The use of technology can also be included on their 504.

One drawback to the 504 plan is that your child will be ineligible to receive any type of specialized instruction, such as one-on-one reading or math help. They also would be unable to receive occupational, physical, or speech therapy.

IEP

The school can screen your child for other issues that are often associated with ADHD, such as learning disabilities. Then, if necessary, the school can create an individual education plan (IEP), which would provide specific accommodations and modifications, such as extra time for tests, smaller assignments, a separate test setting, having tests questions read aloud, etc. Shortened assignments and tests might also be an option for your child. Instead of having to do 20 math problems, your child might only have to do ten. Instead of having to take the test with a pen and paper, they can take it online.

An IEP has more stringent requirements than a 504 plan.

In order for your child to qualify for an IEP, they have to have an identified disability with a negative impact on their ability to be successful in the classroom. Not all children who have ADHD will qualify for an IEP.

The IEP has several different aspects to it.

The first component is a summary that provides details about your child's present level of performance in the academic areas that their disability affects. The summary is specific and provides measurable and objective baseline information. For example, they would read at a third grade level fluently and with comprehension 30 percent of the time.

The second component of an IEP is the goals. These goals are SMART goals. SMART stands for specific, measurable, achievable results, and time-limited. This might look like "They will be reading at a third grade level with fluency and comprehension 60 percent of the time within one year. Fluency means that they can pronounce the words at least 90 percent of the time with accuracy. Comprehension means that they can summarize the text and pick out key details accurately 95 percent of the time." There are no questions left regarding what the goal is for your child.

Benchmarks are the third component of the IEP. Your child will be tested periodically over the year to determine whether they are improving toward their goal. These are also specific and measurable. "They will be reading with fluency and comprehension 33 percent of the time in one month."

One of the IDEA's rules state that children with disabilities must be educated in the least restrictive environment. This means that if possible, your child will be in a regular classroom with their peers who do not have any disabilities. The pull out services will be as minimal as possible.

The IEP will provide for your child to have access to assistive technology if needed. This is important because although some resources are free and you would have access to them at home, other technologies will be more costly. The school receives specific funds for the special education department that pay for the technology, including programs and equipment.

In addition, the IEP will also provide a description for the types of special education services your child will receive and how often. This includes the amount of time they will be pulled from the general classroom so they can receive services separately. For example, if they need help with reading in order to meet their goal, the IEP will state that they will receive two and a half hours of special education services each week. Each session will last for one half hour.

The IEP plan is reviewed each year. You will meet with their general education teacher, the principal, and the special education teacher. Often, the school counselor will attend. If your child receives any other type of therapy, such as speech, that therapist will also attend.

The team will review the IEP and determine whether your child has met their goals. This information will be backed up with evidence. Then, you will work together to make new goals.

Your child will be retested every three years to determine whether they are still eligible for services.

In order to determine whether your child is eligible for an IEP, you have to first document any troubles they are having at school. This might include poor grades, behavior issues, or other problems that affect their success at school. You would schedule a meeting with their teachers to determine what issues they are having in the classroom.

Once the issues have been documented, then your child can be tested to determine whether they have any learning disabilities accompanying their ADHD. You would then contact their school and request that they be assessed to determine whether they qualify for receiving special education services. If they are denied, you do have the right to contest their decision.

If your child does qualify, then you can research different accommodations and modifications available through the IEP. Afterward, the IEP plan is created.

Behavior Intervention Plan

A behavior intervention plan is created by you, your child's teachers, and other educators to help them with their behavior issues at school. Behavior issues can disrupt not only your child's learning, but also that of their classmates. The behavior intervention plan (BIP) is a formal plan that works toward preventing that negative behavior.

There are three parts to a BIP. The first part lists the behaviors causing problems in the classroom. Then, the reasons why this negative behavior is happening are analyzed. The third part describes strategies that can be used to help prevent this behavior.

To determine why the negative behaviors are occurring, a functional behavior assessment will be conducted. The school officials would talk to your child and you to learn your thoughts and feelings regarding the behavior. They would look at your child's school record to find out what other teachers and officials have noticed. If they believe it is necessary, they may test your child for disabilities or other issues that could be causing the negative behavior, such as oppositional defiant disorder.

Using the information they have discovered, the school officials, you, and your child will work to create interventions that will help prevent the negative behavior. These interventions could include moving their seating, changing classrooms, or actions. It might also put in a reward. For example, if your child can sit in their seat during silent reading time at least three days during the week, then they can have a ten-minute extra recess time on Friday.

You can also receive a daily report card that shows what your child has achieved during the day, and they can get stickers or checkmarks on their home chart, helping them earn rewards for their good behavior at home.

A BIP is sometimes included with a 504 plan orIEP if it is determined that their behavior may be part of what is hindering their education. This is especially true if their behavior has resulted in multiple detentions or if they have been suspended because of their actions.

Just like any plan, it should be reviewed periodically. If the plan is working, then perhaps the goals can be changed. For example, instead of sitting and reading during silent reading time for three day, you can make it four. If the plan doesn't seem to be working, then it would need to be readjusted. You and the team might determine that the reasons behind the behavior were wrong, which means the interventions wouldn't work. For example, if they don't sit still during silent reading time because they are embarrassed that their reading level isn't the same as their classmates, then a reward for sitting still may not be effective.

It is important to review the BIP periodically, even if it is working. Some rewards will eventually get old and no longer be effective.

Technology

There are several technological tools that can help your child be successful in class, many of which are free.

Computers are a huge help for students who struggle with ADHD. Your child can type their assignments, which is great, especially if their handwriting is hard to read.

Some students struggle with putting their thoughts onto paper. By the time they type one part of their thought, they already forgot what else they were going to say. Text to speech is a great tool that can help your child speak their thoughts, and the words will be typed on the computer screen for them.

Word prediction tools are also available. As your child types their answers, the program will predict which words would likely come next.

Talking calculators can help your child with math problems. The calculator reads out loud each number or key as it is pressed, as well as the answers.

There are a lot of books, short stories, and articles that can be read aloud. Many common sites that the teachers already use, such as CommonLit or NewsELA have functions that read the texts to the students. Audiobooks are also great tools for students who struggle with reading.

You can talk to your child's teacher about allowing them to use these tools.

Headphones

Headphones can be a great help for students who suffer from ADHD. First, there are noise reduction headphones that can help block out extra noise. This can help reduce the chaos in the environment and keep them focused.

Some children learn better when they listen to music. Allowing students to listen to music while working on assignments can help them stay focused. They won't be able to hear any distractions in the classroom as well.

Chunking

Teachers can also help your child break down large assignments into smaller chunks. For example, if there is a larger research project, your child might be overwhelmed by the idea of all that it entails and simply shut down. However, their teacher can break it into bite-sized tasks. First, your child can choose a topic. Then, they can write down three questions they want to research. As they complete each task, they can check off that particular task. Not only will it prevent the project from being overwhelming, but they can also achieve a sense of accomplishment by successfully completing each smaller step.

Structure and Organization

Organization is important to many children who suffer from ADHD. In order for your child to be more successful in the classroom and not have meltdowns because of unexpected changes, the teacher should let them know when there are changes. In addition, their teacher should also let them know when the class is going to change from one activity to another.

Rules and Expectations

Clearly defined classroom rules are also important. Your child needs to know what is expected of them and the consequences if they don't follow the rules. A 504 plan or BIP can also provide a template for the same reward system that you have created at home. As your child completes specific tasks well, they will get rewards. This may include raising their hand before they speak, staying in their chair when required, and staying on task for a specific amount of time. These can be rewarded as a chart in the classroom or on a daily report card sent home by their teacher. The classroom is hectic, especially at the end of the day, so you can work with the teacher to devise a system that would not add extra stress on them. For example, it could simply be a smaller version of the chart, and the teacher would initial the boxes next to the good behavior.

Your child can work with his teacher to establish nonverbal signals to help him follow the rules. For example, a simple toe tap might remind them that they need to be paying attention. A quiet shake of the head might indicate they need to quit talking to their neighbor about the new video game that has come out. The nonverbal signals will not only prevent class from being further disrupted, but it will also keep your child from feeling as though they are being called out and embarrassed.

Pre-correcting and prompting is another strategy that can be used. For example, the teacher might say, "We are going to read silently now for ten minutes. You should stay in your chair and read your book during this time." Then, prompting would be "Remember, we are sitting and reading silently right now."

Your child's teacher should also praise them when they do well. The praise should be specific so they know exactly what they did that was good.

Clear and Explicit Instructions

The teacher should provide clear and explicit instructions, since children with ADHD struggle to understand and follow through with instructions. The teacher should then ask them to repeat the instructions back to the teacher.

The instructions should be written someplace where your child can easily see them and be reminded of what they are supposed to do. If they do get off task, then the teacher can easily point to what your child is supposed to be doing and redirect them.

Guided Notes

Guided notes are a huge help to children who are struggling academically. These are notes with a lot of the information that the teacher is lecturing about. They can be fill-in-the-blank notes, so your child would have to pay attention and listen for the keyword to put in the blank. They could be multiple choice, so they have to circle the correct answer.

Another great note system for younger people is doodle notes. This is a notetaking system with visuals that correlate with the information being taught. For example, if the teacher is talking about the different parts of the flower, then the doodle notes might have a picture of the flower that your child can color and label. This technique requires your child to use both hemispheres of their brain, which helps them be more focused and remember the information better.

The teacher can also provide the notes to your child ahead of time or put them in a Google Classroom, or some other virtual classroom.

You can also ask the teacher if your child can record the lessons. Not only will that let them go back and listen to the information as many times as they need to, but it will also help you understand the lesson when you are helping them with homework.

Alternate Seated and Non-Seated Activities

Your child's teacher can also help them manage their hyperactivity by alternating between high energy and low energy activities. This gives them the chance to get some of that excess energy out while staying on task, and it also creates a better chance for them to stay on task during the low energy activities.

Likewise, hands-on activities, such as project-based learning, will help your child stay on task. Although this is not always possible, it is an option when the teacher allows it.

Special Seating

Wobble chairs, standing desks, pedals, and other types of accommodations might help soothe your child's restlessness. In addition, their teacher might allow them to stand up and walk behind the rest of their classmates, as long as they aren't interfering with their classmates' learning.

Stress Balls

Letting your child have a stress ball that they can squeeze when they start to get anxious or frustrated can help stop negative reactions. It would also give them a moment to pause and think about their feelings, thoughts, and possible reactions, while considering what the consequences for negative reactions would be.

Weighted Vests

Like weighted blankets, weighted vests mimic the feelings of deep pressure stimulation. Research suggests that if your child wears a weighted vest, they will likely leave their seat less and fidget less. They would also be able to focus on their tasks better.

Movement

There are a lot of ways the teacher can give your child an opportunity to move around in class without getting in trouble or disrupting their classmates. There are usually jobs they can do to help out, such as handing back graded assignments, picking up completed work that the class is working on, or handing out supplies. Teachers might also have their own ways to handle antsy children, such as giving them a folder that needs to be delivered to another teacher. The other teacher would take the folder and whatever is inside, write a quick thank you note, and send the folder back to their classroom teacher.

It is a good bet that your child is not the only one in the room with ants in their pants. Their teacher can have the class do ten jumping jacks between assignments. Other assignments can have these movements built in. Talk to your child's teacher to see what they can arrange for your child. It might also help if you have some options that you can kindly suggest to the teacher.

Summer and Afterschool Programs

There are many summer programs that can prove beneficial to your child. They usually consist of both academic activities, as well as simply fun activities. The summer programs, designed for children with ADHD, often include different treatment elements that are very effective for these children. This includes parent training for behavior modification practices. Positive reinforcement—using tokens or points—are also usually involved in the summer programs, as well as consequences, such as timeouts. In addition, counselors use effective commands, issue daily report cards, provide training for social skills, and have sports skills training. The counselors would also teach the children effective problem solving skills.

Research indicates that children with ADHD who attend these types of summer programs grow a lot in areas that they struggled with in the past. The camp helps the children improve their relationships with their peers, how they interact with adults, and in academics. Because of these improvements, their self-confidence improves.

AFTERWORD

Let your child know that you believe in them. Set high goals for them and tell them that you know they will be able to achieve them. Celebrate their successes. Even when times are hard and their teacher calls for the third time that week, let your child know that you love them and believe in them.

Work with your child's teacher and other school staff to find the best ways to help them be successful. If their ADHD or other learning disabilities are preventing them from being successful in the classroom, then you can advocate for them to be tested and see if they are eligible for a 504 plan or IEP. If behavior continues to be a problem, then you can work with the school to create a behavior intervention plan.

It is important to communicate with their teachers to discuss how they can help your child be successful, from preferred seating, to guided notes, or even weighted vests. Afterschool and summer programs can also be great resources to help your child be successful.

Chapter Summary

- School is a significant issue for children with ADHD.
- There are several ways you can help your child at home be successful in school.
- Work with your child's teachers and other school staff to create a plan to help ensure your child's success.

In the next chapter, you will learn how a healthy diet can help your child.

CHAPTER SIX: A HEALTHY DIET

*N*utrition is a key component in everyone's health. It is especially important for a child who suffers from ADHD.

Vitamins, minerals, and other key ingredients in foods and beverages can have a profound effect on the brain and body. The amount of food and timing of meals is also very important.

Your child's diet can have a profound effect on their symptoms of ADHD. The right diet can help decrease their hyperactivity and impulsiveness, and improve their calmness and ability to focus.

With so many myths regarding what is healthy and not, it can be very intimidating to try to find the best foods for your child. However, there are some basic tips that can help you.

Food to Eat

If they have a waffle and orange juice or a pop tart for breakfast, their sugar levels are going to go through the roof. They will crash in time for lunch. If their lunch consists of a lot of carbohydrates and sugars and very little protein, then the cycle will start all over again.

To avoid this, your child should have meals with more protein, fiber, and complex carbs. Oatmeal and a glass of milk for breakfast is great. If they won't eat the oatmeal, then some peanut butter toast will do the trick. The protein and fiber will cause the carbs from the bread to be digested slower so the sugar rush isn't an issue. This will help them concentrate better at school, and their behavior will be better.

Protein-Rich Food

Foods that are rich in protein can have a positive effect on your child. The brain uses protein to create neurotransmitters, which are chemicals that help your cells talk to each other. Protein is also helpful because it can prevent blood sugar spikes.

A breakfast high in protein can help your child focus better in class and be less hyperactive and impulsive.

Soy, eggs, fish, beans, nuts, pork, poultry, and lean beef are all great sources of protein. Bring on the bacon and eggs!

Apples

"An apple a day keeps the doctor away." Interestingly enough, apples can also help keep the symptoms of ADHD away.. Doctors recommend that children who suffer from ADHD consume a lot of complex carbohydrates because they help improve symptoms of ADHD. One great source of complex carbohydrates are apples. Another great benefit of eating apples, especially right before bed, is that they have been shown to help children sleep better.

Goat Cheese

Cheese has a lot of calcium and protein, which all children need. Cheese also helps improve your child's concentration and improve how their ADHD medications work. However, if your child is lactose intolerant, eating cheese made from cow's milk can make their ADHD symptoms worse. Goat cheese may be the perfect replacement.

Pears

Pears don't have a great rhyme to go with them, but they do have a lot of the same benefits. They are a great source of complex carbohydrates. Like apples, eating pears right before bed can help your child get a good night's sleep.

. . .

Tuna

Tuna is a terrific source of omega-3 fatty acids, which has been proven to help reduce symptoms of ADHD. Tuna can be used for wraps, sandwiches, and pasta salads.

Eggs

Eggs have a lot of protein, which is important for helping children who suffer from ADHD. Eating a lot of eggs can help your child with their concentration and enhance the effectiveness of ADHD medications. If you don't have a lot of time in the morning to make eggs, you can always hard boil them and have them ready for the morning.

Nuts

Nuts are also a great source of omega-3 fatty acids. Studies indicate that walnuts and Brazil nuts have the best impact as far as managing your child's symptoms. However, almonds have been shown to have a great effect as well.

Spinach

Most kids turn their noses up when they hear the word. However, spinach is at the top of the list when it comes to foods that help control ADHD symptoms. It doesn't have to come in a can. Fresh spinach is great on salads. If your child still refuses to eat it, then sneak it in a blender with some strawberries and bananas. They'll never know they're getting this maligned vegetable along with their yummy treat.

Oranges and 100% Pure Orange Juice

Oranges are another fruit that proves to be a great source of complex carbohydrates. Like pears and apples, they are a great way to help your child fall asleep, which can be an issue for children who suffer from ADHD. In addition, oranges are full of vitamin C. They not only help improve your child's ADHD symptoms, but they also help build up their immunity.

. . .

Kiwi

It sounds like you need to have a fruit salad—with kiwi on top. Kiwis are rich in complex carbohydrates, which are important for helping your child control their ADHD symptoms.

Salmon

Salmon, like tuna, is a great source of omega-3 fatty acids. It is also one of the healthiest fish you can feed your family. Including salmon on your menu at least once a week will help improve many of the symptoms of ADHD.

Whole Grain Cereal

It's not just kids who love Fruit Loops and Lucky Charms. Unfortunately, these cereals are not good for your child. Not only are they loaded with sugar, but they also have dyes, artificial sweeteners, and artificial flavors that can make your child's ADHD symptoms a lot worse.

Instead, choose the whole grain cereal. Whole grain or multigrain Cheerios are definitely a good choice. Instead of adding a lot of sugar to them, you can add some fruit to sweeten up breakfast.

White Fish

White fish are also a good source for omega-3 fatty acids. When you get tired of salmon and tuna, you might opt for some cod, tilapia, snapper, haddock, grouper, bass, or catfish. They can be used in a variety of recipes that your family won't get tired of soon.

Beans

Beans are a great source of protein as well. Kidney beans, pinto beans, and all other kinds of beans are great for helping your child's brain increase its production of dopamine and control their ADHD symptoms.

Grapefruit

Although they are a little sour, grapefruit is another good source of complex carbohydrates. A glass of 100 percent juice to accompany the eggs and bacon for breakfast would help your child manage their ADHD symptoms throughout the day. A snack at night can help them get a good night's rest.

Chicken

Chicken is one of the best sources of protein. The great thing about chicken is that there are so many different ways you can prepare it that your family never has to eat the same meal twice.

Other Foods that Are a Good Source of Complex Carbohydrates

In addition to a lot of fruit, there are other foods that are a rich source of complex carbohydrates. Barley, maple water, popcorn, quinoa, chickpeas, beans, brown rice, whole grain bread and pasta, and sweet potatoes are all good choices.

Foods, Preservatives, and Chemicals to Avoid

There are many foods, preservatives, and chemicals that your child should avoid because they have a negative effect on the symptoms of ADHD.

A lot of these are found in the form of additives and preservatives in the foods, as well as artificial colors. This means that you have to take a lot of time to read labels when you go grocery shopping, at least until you get a standard grocery list going.

Of course, buying fresh processed foods will be the best bet when you are looking for groceries without additives and preservatives. The bad thing about these foods is that they are generally more expensive. They are also less loved by your children.

The good news is that there are many different types of foods that you can find in the store that are additive and preservative-free simply because many people are trying to live healthier. These include favorites such as pizza, certain cereals, cookies, among other foods.

It is important to know what you should avoid, so that, as your child puts them on your grocery list, you can cross them right off.

Carbohydrates and Simple Sugars

This is definitely easier said than done. So many foods geared toward kids are loaded with sugar. All you have to do is take a walk down the cereal aisle to know that. Plus, kids do love their candy, soda, and other sugary treats.

Unfortunately, these types of foods can make the symptoms of your child's ADHD even worse. The spike in sugar increases their energy. They'll be bouncing off the walls for quite a while. That is, until the insulin levels increase drastically to counterbalance the sudden increase of their blood sugar levels. Then, the sugar crash happens because their blood sugar levels are too low. Then, they are lethargic, grumpy, and stressed out. Neither scenario is good for controlling their hyperactivity, impulsiveness, or ability to pay attention and focus on the tasks at hand.

Dyes

Many dyes found in a lot of foods and drinks are thought to be the culprit in making symptoms of ADHD worse. The dyes are used to add color to drinks, especially those with no flavor. They also enhance colors to make them more attractive. Manufacturers will often add dyes to foods and drinks to prevent them from losing colors because of environmental issues, such as sitting on a shelf for long periods of time or being exposed to bright lights or the sun.

The FDA approves all of the dyes used in consumable products. However, because of the ingredients, there may be elements that affect ADHD symptoms.

Some dyes are created from natural products, such as fats and oils. However, dyes are also created with chemicals. A lot of the coloring agents that seem to cause trouble for people suffering from ADHD are created artificially. The main suspects are red #3, red #40, blue #2, yellow #5, and yellow #6. These, as well as sodium benzoate, have been shown in studies to increase hyperactivity and inattentiveness in children.

Specific Foods to Avoid

Candy

Children love candy. Unfortunately, children who suffer from ADHD should definitely avoid it. First, it is loaded with simple sugars, which can cause their blood sugar to spike, then crash, thus making the ADHD symptoms worse.

Second, a lot of candy has artificial colors and flavors that can contribute to hyperactivity and impulsive actions.

Sodas, Caffeine, and High Fructose Corn Syrup

Sodas are another source of simple sugar. Many sodas also contain caffeine, which increases hyperactivity, impulsivity, and the inability to focus on tasks at hand. In addition, one study indicated that children who drank sodas were more inclined to be irritable and aggressive. They also tended to withdraw socially from their peers.

Frozen Fruit and Vegetables

"But fruits and vegetables are good for my child." They are. However, some frozen fruits and vegetables have dyes added to them to make sure they keep their color while frozen. You need to read the labels to find the brands that don't add extra coloring.

Another issue with frozen fruits and vegetables is that some of them are treated with organophosphates, which is an insecticide. Studies have shown that this chemical can cause neurologic-based problems with behavior.

Cake Mixes and Frosting

One problem with cake mixes and frosting is that they contain high amounts of simple sugars. Many of them also have a large amount of artificial sweeteners, which can cause even more problems for children with ADHD.

Ice Cream

Dairy products, such as this tasty treat, can increase the symptoms of ADHD, especially if your child has a hypersensitivity to milk products.

. . .

Yogurt

Yogurt is another one of those tasty treats that your child should avoid. You can try these foods for a while to see if they do increase your child's symptoms. If this food does seem to exacerbate the symptoms, then you can try switching to soy products.

Energy Drinks

Energy drinks are a big problem for kids with ADHD. They are popular, but unfortunately, they have a lot of ingredients that are bad for children with ADHD. Caffeine is one chemical that causes a lot of problems for kids with ADHD. It also has a lot of artificial sweeteners, which can all also cause a lot of problems for those who suffer from ADHD.

Coffee

Coffee is another popular drink that kids shouldn't indulge in. The caffeine makes it a problem. However, if your child would like a healthy, energetic start to their day with a "grown up" drink, then they could try some green tea or other herbal teas.

Chocolate

Chocolate also has a lot of caffeine and will trigger ADHD symptoms. If your child does like a chocolatey treat, you might opt for some white chocolate instead.

Frozen Pizza

Unfortunately, this standby for hectic nights is not a good choice for your child with ADHD. They are loaded with artificial colors and flavors, which will only make your child's symptoms worse. You can always make your own pizza if it is a family favorite. It can still be a quick dinner if you prepare all the ingredients ahead of time.

Corn

There seems to be an issue with the color yellow because yellow vegetables, such as corn and yellow squash, also seem to be a problem for kids with ADHD.

Bananas don't fit into this restriction, because only the peel is yellow. The fruit that you eat is actually white.

Chips

It will seem that you are having to restrict all the delicious snacks that your child loves, but unfortunately, chips need to be added to the list. They are loaded with artificial colors and flavors. Vegetables and other healthy foods are a much better snack.

Fruit Juices that Aren't 100%

A lot of fruit juices have artificial colors and flavors in them, as well as preservatives. Read the labels and avoid any juices or fruit cocktails that have the following ingredients: high fructose corn syrup, molasses, malt syrup, maltodextrin, dextrose, dextrin, or dehydrated cane juice. All of these ingredients are nothing more than sugar with an alias.

Fast Food

This one really hurts, but unfortunately, fast food is at the top of the no-no list. The fried foods that are a staple of fast food only exacerbate the symptoms of ADHD. There are loads of artificial flavoring and colors, as well as preservatives and additives.

Certain Cereals

There are a lot of cereals that should be crossed off the grocery list because they contain artificial flavors and colors. They also contain sodium benzoate, which is a preservative that makes some children who suffer from ADHD even more hyperactive. This means that Trix aren't for kids, and Lucky Charms, Fruity Pebbles, and Fruit Loops are also off the menu.

Other Foods to Avoid

There are other foods that you should limit for your child, as they contain simple carbohydrates. White bread, white rice, white pasta, sports drinks, and potatoes without the skins are included in this list.

The Ideal Plate

With all of the dos and don'ts that seem to be attached to meal times, what does the ideal dinner plate look like? Dr. Ned Hallowell, founder of Hallowell Center for Cognitive and Emotional health said that half the plate should have fruits and vegetables. A quarter of the plate should have protein-based food, while the other quarter should have carbohydrates (such as beans or legumes).

Test for Food Reactions

Every child is different, and every child will have a different reaction to dyes, additives, and preservatives. Although some children might start bouncing off walls just by hearing the words "Mountain Dew," your child might be able to drink a two-liter with a chocolate bar and not move a muscle for hours.

The key is to test for food reactions. Start with a few basic foods, such as chicken, oatmeal, and others that are known to make the symptoms of ADHD worse. Then, gradually add different food to see if your child's behavior changes.

While they're eating a regular diet, make a note of their behavior. Monitor their hyperactivity and impulsivity levels, as well as their ability to concentrate on lessons.

Then, once you have established a baseline, you can gradually add foods to see if anything changes. For example, if ice cream was one of their favorite foods in the past, and you want to see if it would make a difference, then you can offer some to them and monitor their behavior. If it doesn't seem to have an effect, then an occasional frosty treat would be perfectly fine without any negative repercussions.

AFTERWORD

Life is tough enough without having to worry about every single ingredient in every single food item that you buy. Unfortunately, it is one of the necessary evils that accompany all other precautions you must take when you have a child with ADHD.

There are many foods and drinks that they should not be eating because they will make their symptoms worse. On the other hand, there are a lot of tasty foods that can help significantly improve their ADHD symptoms.

The great news is that by helping your child control their ADHD, the entire family can benefit by eating healthier, tastier meals.

Chapter Summary

- Nutrition has a huge impact on children with ADHD.
- Foods high in protein and complex carbohydrates can help significantly improve the symptoms of ADHD.
- There are many foods that should be avoided, especially those that contain simple sugars, simple carbohydrates, artificial dyes and sweeteners, and other additives and preservatives.

In the next chapter, you will learn about natural remedies and supplements.

CHAPTER SEVEN: SUPPLEMENTS, VITAMINS, MINERALS, AND HERBS

There are a lot of vitamins and minerals that have been shown to improve ADHD symptoms. There are some, like complex carbohydrates and proteins, that you can get from diets. Others, such as the omega-3 fatty acids that help the brain cells and rest of the body function well, are not always provided adequately by food. Because ADHD is a brain disability, the foods your child eats, as well as other supplements, can have a significant impact on them.

Before you go this route, you should talk to your doctor to get more information. There are some questions you can ask them.

The first one is how supplements would improve your child's attention, impulsiveness, and hyperactivity. Although research has been done on all the supplements, vitamins, minerals, and herbs mentioned in this chapter, and have been shown to be effective in helping improve symptoms, it is important to remember that every child is different.

Another question to consider is how effective the supplements are. They are usually not considered as a replacement for medication because they do not work as quickly nor have as great an effect. One upside to them is that they do not have as many side effects, and if they do, they are not as severe.

The length of time it takes for the supplements to take effect is another question that you could address with your child's doctor. In general, the time it will take will depend on which supplement you are discussing, and as always, your child, since every person is different. For example, one doctor said that some of her patients said they saw a difference within a couple of days of starting omega-3 supplements, whereas others didn't see a difference at all even after a month.

An important consideration for supplements is the side effects. There are some supplements that will have side effects, although they tend to be less severe and happen less often than those of ADHD medications. If your child does experience any side effects, you should stop giving the supplements to them immediately and contact their doctor.

Supplements

Health nuts and athletes are not the only people who can benefit from supplements. There are many supplements that affect people physically, mentally, and emotionally. A lot of these supplements have profound positive effects for children with ADHD.

Fish Oil

Sounds disgusting, doesn't it? However, fish oil is an important part of your child's nutritional needs. According to Dr. William Sears, the more of these types of healthy fats in the diet, the better because they make up 60 percent of the brain and nerves that power everything in the body. Omega-3s, which are found in fish oil, have been shown to help improve symptoms of ADHD. People who consume omega-3s can decrease their hyperactivity and impulsiveness and improve their concentration.

According to Dr. Sandy Newmark, there have been many studies that have shown that these supplements can have profound effects on children with ADHD. She said that there was one study, conducted in Sweden, that researched the effect that fish oil had on children with ADHD. After taking the supplement for three months, 25 percent of the children showed a significant improvement in their symptoms. Almost 50 percent of the children showed a huge decrease in their ADHD-related symptoms after six months.

Omega-3s are essential fats for the brain to function normally. Your body does not produce them, so you have to get these fats from your food. According to some research, children who suffer from ADHD have much lower levels of the necessary omega-3s than their counterparts who do not have the disability.

Of course, your child can get these omega-3s from eating fish. However, most people don't eat enough fish to get what they need. Therefore, they have to take supplements. There are regular supplements that come in the form of a pill. However, there are other supplements made for kids, and those who tried them said they actually taste pretty good.

Iron

Iron is another mineral that children who suffer from ADHD are often lacking. Studies have indicated that children with ADHD generally have half of what their peers do. The children with lower iron levels were not anemic; they simply had a decreased amount of iron in their blood.

Other studies have indicated that increasing iron levels in your child's body can have a significant effect on symptoms associated with ADHD.

Iron plays an important role in the body. It delivers oxygen to your muscles and cells. It has an important role in the brain too because it helps in the production of dopamine, which as you know, is low in people with ADHD.

In addition, iron can decrease the occurrences of restless leg syndrome, which is a problem that people with ADHD often have. This syndrome, characterized by tingling or a feeling of something crawling in the legs, often occurs at night, preventing your child from getting a good night's rest.

Iron can be increased by supplements. Before you start your child on a supplement, you should first have their iron levels checked by their doctor. If the iron levels—also referred to as ferritin—are below 35, then a supplement would be safe.

It can also be increased by having your child eat more poultry, lean red meat, shellfish, and beans. It is also found in other types of iron-fortified foods, such as Cheerios, Wheaties, peas, bananas, peanut butter, baked potatoes, and whole wheat bread.

Food that is high in vitamin C, such as oranges or grapefruits, can help your child absorb iron.

Zinc and Magnesium

As with the other minerals and vitamins, zinc and magnesium are important for everyone, and a lot of people do not have enough of it. It has also been shown to improve the symptoms of ADHD.

Zinc is important because it helps regulate dopamine and the brain be more responsive to the dopamine. Because of this, it may help make certain ADHD medications, such as methylphenidate, more effective.

Magnesium is also important in the creation of neurotransmitters that affect concentration and attention. It also helps calm the brain.

There are many foods that provide these minerals. Pumpkin seeds, almonds, spinach, peanuts, cashews, soy milk, bananas, brown rice, carrots, and apples are just a few of the foods that are rich in magnesium. Meat, seeds, chickpeas, cocoa powder, cashews, mushrooms, and spinach are all great sources of zinc.

If you and your doctor determine that your child isn't getting enough of either of these minerals, then another option is that they can take supplements to boost their levels.

Vitamins that Affect Learning and Behavior

Vitamin C—Your brain needs vitamin C to make neurotransmitters. This vitamin is so essential that the brain uses a special pump to draw vitamin C from the blood.

Vitamin B6–A lack of vitamin B6 can make your child grumpier and more fatigued. This vitamin helps increase the brain's levels of dopamine, which increases alertness and helps your child focus and concentrate better.

Vitamin D—Many people have very low levels of vitamin D. Research indicates that children who suffer from ADHD have even lower levels of Vitamin D than their peers. Vitamin D is important because it helps regulate the amount of calcium and phosphates in the body. Research studies have shown that vitamin D supplements helped children with ADHD decrease their inattention, hyperactivity, and negative behaviors. It increased the children's ability to focus and concentrate on their tasks.

Inositol

Inositol is a vitamin-like element that is present in several different foods. In larger doses, this substance can help reduce agitation and anxiety.

Melatonin

Melatonin is a hormone that your body produces to help you sleep. After your child has brushed their teeth and you've read them their bedtime story, tucked them into bed, and turned off their light, their body would naturally begin producing this hormone, which should cause them to feel sleepy. However, sometimes, it isn't enough, and your child struggles to fall asleep. A melatonin supplement might help them get to sleep. It is also safe to use in moderation.

Herbs

There are many herbs thought to help improve symptoms of ADHD. Most of the natural and herbal remedies are not approved by the FDA, although there is research to suggest that they are effective.

Ginkgo and Ginseng

Ginkgo and ginseng are known to activate cognitive abilities. They increase levels of dopamine and norepinephrine levels in the brain. Usually, those who take these two herbs see an improvement in their ADHD symptoms and are less impulsive. They are also able to focus and concentrate better.

Pycnogenol

This is an extract from French maritime pine bark. Studies have shown that it decreases hyperactivity and helped improve attention, concentration, and motor-coordination in students after they took the herb for one month. The herb has a large number of polyphenols, which are antioxidants that help protect brain cells from being damaged by free radicals.

Rhodiola Rosea

This herb is made from a plant grown in the Arctic. It has shown to help improve attention, alertness, and accuracy.

Valerian

Many children who suffer from ADHD have a difficult time going to and staying asleep. Valerian is an herb that has been shown to decrease hyperactivity and anxiety. In addition, it can help with your child's sleep problems. It can also decrease the rebound effect that some children may have once their stimulant medication wears off.

Passion flower

Passion flowers have benefits that can help reduce symptoms of ADHD. One benefit is that it can help your child get a good night's rest. It may also reduce some of their other symptoms, such as hyperactivity and impulsivity, while improving concentration and focus.

Lemon Balm

One study that involved 169 children showed that lemon balm, combined with valerian, had a significant impact on reducing symptoms caused by ADHD. The study observed the number of children who suffered from an inability to concentrate decreasing from 75 percent to 14 percent. The number of participants who suffered from hyperactivity decreased from 61 percent to 13 percent. Participants who suffered from impulsivity decreased from 59 percent to 22 percent. In addition, the study indicated that their social behavior and sleep habits improved. Stress levels due to their ADHD symptoms also decreased.

AFTERWORD

There are many vitamins and minerals that are essential to good health. Many times, these are an especially important concern when discussing children who suffer from ADHD. Although medication is often a good answer, certain supplements and herbs can help decrease the effect of ADHD.

Before you start any supplement or other regime, you should talk with your child's doctor to make sure they are given the right dose and the supplements will be helpful. Remember that each person is different and will react differently to any changes in their nutrition or supplements. If your child shows signs of being allergic to anything, or if they start showing side effects, you should contact their doctor immediately.

Chapter Summary

- There are many supplements and herbs that can help your child manage their ADHD symptoms.
- It is important to research these elements and talk to your child's doctor before giving them to your child.
- Remember that everyone reacts differently to supplements and natural remedies.

In the next chapter, you will learn various health tips.

8

CHAPTER EIGHT: HEALTH AND YOUR CHILD
WITH ADHD

*H*ealth is an important consideration for all people, regardless of whether they suffer from ADHD. However, it can be especially important for children with ADHD. There is a direct correlation between the body and mind. The more fit the body is, the healthier the mind will be.

One reason that health is an especially important concern for ADHD children is that it has a direct effect on the child and vice versa.

Sleep

You've read bedtime stories. You've gotten them four drinks of water and they went to the bathroom five times. They've been in bed for more than an hour, but they still aren't asleep. It's late, you are tired, but they're wide awake.

There is a clear link between the inability to fall asleep and ADHD are evident.

One problem that might cause insomnia is that people with ADHD struggle to "turn off their brain." Thoughts bounce around in their minds nonstop. Another problem is that once your child falls asleep, they might have trouble staying asleep. Children who suffer from ADHD tend to have more nightmares, wet the bed more often, and have other sleeping problems, such as restless leg syndrome.

If you've ever stayed up all night to finish a last-minute homework assignment or just watch movies, you know that not getting enough sleep the night before can make mornings dreadful. You have trouble focusing and resisting distractions. You are also grumpier. At least I am.

There is an important correlation between health and sleep. First, there is a direct correlation between a good, restful sleep and the ability to pay sustained attention the next day, as well as regulating mood. In addition, a good night's sleep has a significant impact on learning, as the information learned during the day is replayed and absorbed through an active brain at night.

There are several ways you can help your child get to sleep easier and stay asleep, so they can be rested and ready for school the next day.

Food and Drink

Complex Carbohydrates

As discussed in the food section, fruit is a great source of complex carbohydrates, as is peanut butter, granola, and yogurt. There are two reasons why these foods can help your child sleep. One is that the complex carbohydrates send tryptophan to the brain. This is an amino acid that makes people sleepy. The second reason is that complex carbohydrates take a long time to digest. This means that all their energy is focused on the digestion process, making them tired. This is why everyone wants to take a long siesta after eating a big meal.

The added bonus of eating peanut butter is that it is rich in proteins. The proteins aid in stabilizing blood sugar during the night, helping your child sleep better.

Protein

Protein is one element that can help your child sleep better. Protein helps to keep blood sugar stable throughout the night. Protein, in general, has been shown to help people sleep better through the night.

Dairy Products

A glass of milk, yogurt, or cottage cheese may help your child fall asleep faster and stay asleep better because they contain tryptophan.

. . .

Turkey

Have you ever eaten a big turkey dinner and felt sleepy? The reason, besides how all your energy is digesting food, is because turkey has the amino acid tryptophan. This amino acid increases your body's production of melatonin.

Almonds

Almonds can help your child sleep better for a couple of reasons. One is that almonds are a good source of melatonin. It also is a great source of magnesium, which is not only an important mineral for children with ADHD, but it also helps improve the quality of their sleep. One reason for this is that magnesium reduces the hormone cortisol. Cortisol, like adrenaline, is released when you feel stressed, helping to prompt the fight or flight reaction.

Chamomile Tea

This beverage is terrific for several reasons. One is that it has a lot of antioxidants to help reduce your risk for cancer and heart disease. It can also help improve your immune system. Chamomile tea can help your child get to sleep and sleep better for a couple of reasons. One is that it helps with their anxiety and depression if applicable. The tea also has apigenin, which is an antioxidant that binds to specific brain receptors that increase sleepiness.

Kiwi

According to Kathy Warwick, a registered dietician, kiwi is one of the best foods your child can eat before going to bed. Studies have shown that people who ate two kiwis before bed fell asleep 42 percent quicker than those who didn't. In addition, their ability to stay asleep throughout the night increased by 5 percent. Their total sleep time increased by 13 percent.

Kiwis have anti-inflammatory antioxidants, such as carotenoids, which help improve sleep. They also are rich in vitamin C and serotonin. Serotonin is a neurotransmitter hormone that helps stabilize moods, feelings of well-being, and happiness.

. . .

Tart Cherry Juice

Tart cherry juice has been known to promote sleepiness and relieve insomnia. It has a large amount of melatonin. Studies found that people suffering from insomnia who drank eight ounces of tart cherry juice twice a day for two weeks slept about 84 minutes longer and said that they slept better than usual.

Fatty Fish

As well as the other benefits described in the nutrition chapter, fatty fish such as tuna, trout, salmon, and mackerel have high amounts of omega-3 fatty acids and vitamin D. This combination increases the quality of sleep. In addition, fatty fish has shown to improve the production of serotonin.

Walnuts

Walnuts have high amounts of fatty acids, which contribute to improving your quality of sleep. The nuts have alpha linoleic acid and omega-3 fatty acids. These two acids combine to DHA, which, in turn, increases the production of serotonin.

Passion Flower Tea

Passion flower tea has been proven to reduce anxiety. It contains the antioxidant apigenin, which calms your brain. In addition, passion flower tea increases your brain's production of gamma aminobutyric acid, which helps reduce the production of stress-producing brain chemicals, such as glutamate. It will help calm your child and promote sleepiness.

Bananas

Who doesn't love bananas? The great news is that this favorite treat can help your child sleep, since they are a good source of tryptophan and magnesium.

Oatmeal

Oatmeal contains complex carbohydrates that can help your child sleep. In addition, oatmeal has more fiber and is a good source of melatonin. The oatmeal doesn't have to be in the form of the mushy breakfast staple. Oat-based granola bars, especially that with fruit bits, are a great snack for them to have right before bed.

Stick to a Routine

Routines can help train your child's body. If they get into a specific routine, their brain and body will know what to expect next. First, they shower. Then, they brush their teeth. After that, they pick out their clothes. Finally, they slide into bed and read for a certain period of time. ADDitude, the website and magazine for ADD and ADHD, has a suggested evening routine that can help your child get a good night's rest.

You should plan for your child to go to bed early. Children need about ten hours of sleep to be healthy and have a good day.

Then, you can plan what they are having for breakfast and lunch. That avoids any arguments in the morning.

It is a good idea to pack their backpack and have it waiting by the door for them in the morning so they don't forget it.

Another good idea is to have them take their shower or bath at night. First, it helps prevent conflicts in the morning when bathroom time is at a premium. Also, a bath or shower can help them sleep better. If they have a particularly hard time sleeping, a warm bath might help, especially if it has a slight aroma of lavender or chamomile. These scents are known to cause sleepiness and are light-scented, so they won't affect your child's hypersensitivity.

About 30 minutes before bedtime, give your child a protein-rich snack, like peanut butter, cheese, or seeds, or one with complex carbohydrates, such as fruit.

Then, play a quiet game or read a book. It is best if the phones, tablets, and televisions are turned off because the blue light can keep them awake. In addition, playing a game or reading a book together is great for family time.

A goodnight ritual is another way to help your child sleep well. When you give them their goodnight hug and tell them that you love them, it lets their body and brain know that it is time for sleep. It also lets them know they are loved and an important part of the family, even with the chaos.

. . .

Supplements

If at all possible, you should avoid sleeping pills. First, while pills might be safe for adults, they might not be as safe for children. Also, many sleeping pills leave a person feeling drowsy the next day. There are, however, natural elements that can help your child sleep.

Melatonin

Melatonin is a natural hormone produced by your body that lets your brain know it is time to go to sleep and improves your sleep time. This hormone is released based on the time of day (usually), so that is why you would start to get sleepy when it starts to get dark outside.

Melatonin sleep aids are a great way to help your child get sleep when their ADHD is fighting the sandman. You will need to check the label to see which dosage would be right for your child.

Valerian Root

This herb is great for a number of reasons. It is known to help treat depression and anxiety and increases relaxation. It can be taken as a tea, liquid extract, or in a capsule. This root is safe, although some people have said they had dry mouth and vivid dreams. There might be additional side effects if it is taken constantly over a long period of time.

Glycine

This is an amino acid with an important effect on your nervous system. It has been shown to help improve sleep quality. It can be taken as a pill or in powder form. It is also found in a lot of food, such as spinach, fruit, kale, cabbage, meat, eggs, fish, and poultry.

Relaxation Techniques

There are many ways to help your child fall and stay asleep.

Deep Breathing Exercises

Breathing exercises can help your child sleep. As noted in chapter three, breathing exercises can help relax your child. The breathing exercises also help your child focus their mind on nothing else but their breathing, helping calm the chaos.

One great breathing exercise is the five square. Your child should breathe in through their nose for five seconds, hold it for five, and then breathe out for five through their mouth. Then, they would wait another five seconds before repeating the process.

Blackout Curtains

Blackout curtains are a great tool to help your child go to and stay asleep. It is often light out in the spring, summer, and fall, well into the night, and sometimes past their bedtime. Their brain thinks that since it is light outside that they should be awake and doing something. Blackout curtains will help remind their brain it is time to sleep. In addition, if your child is hypersensitive to light, then blackout curtains will make it easier for them to sleep.

The other way that blackout curtains can help is that exposure to too much light can restrict the amount of melatonin that their body produces.

White Noise

A lot of people struggle to sleep if it is noisy. This can be especially true if your child is hypersensitive to sound. They can hear the television going, someone getting a second helping of ice cream, and all the cars going by on the street. These sounds can distract them from getting to sleep. Instead, it has their mind fired up on all six cylinders.

There are many ways to create white noise to prevent these exterior sounds from keeping them awake. A fan or air purifier might make enough noise to drown out everything else. There are also nature sounds that you can play, such as birds, wolves howling, waterfalls, and thunderstorms. They are free on YouTube.

He might also have a favorite song or type of music that he likes to listen to. Although Mega Death might not be a great choice, some of their calmer favorites might lull them to sleep. Even if they are reciting the words in their head, they are focused on the sound and those words, which, in turn, can tame the million other thoughts that are demanding attention.

. . .

Aroma Therapy

There are several scents that are known to help people sleep.

Studies have shown that lavender oil helps people relax and fall asleep. It also helps improve the quality of sleep, which is very important for children who suffer from ADHD. You can put these oils on a diffuser about an hour before bed. You can also put a drop or two on the pillow case or a cotton ball and put it inside the pillow case.

Ylang Ylang smells like rose and jasmine. It is known to relieve tension and stress, as well as cause sleepiness. This oil can be diffused before bedtime or added to a warm bath.

Marjoram is not just for cooking. This oil has a spicy scent with a bit of pepper and has been shown to help cause drowsiness. A drop on the nape of their neck will relieve stress. You can also diffuse it before bed.

Frankincense isn't only a Christmas spice. This oil smells sweet, woody, with a bit of citrus and other spices. This oil is known to relieve stress and help people relax. You can put a couple of drops of this oil into your child's hands and have him rub them together. Then he can inhale the relaxing scent.

Cedarwood, which smells earthy and smoky, has natural sedative properties. It is also known to promote a feeling of being safe. In addition, it also repels bugs and helps fight colds. You can put a couple drops of this oil on your child's pillowcase or on a cotton ball inside their pillowcase.

Neroli has a floral scent with a hint of pepper and orange. This oil is great for people who suffer from insomnia because it helps relax people's minds. It is useful for relieving grief, decreasing blood pressure, and soothing any agitation. You can rub a couple of drops directly into your child's skin.

Chamomile is one of the more common herbs known to help people sleep. It helps relieve anger, grumpiness, and agitation. You can dab a couple of drops on the bottom of your child's feet to help them sleep. As an added bonus, you can give them a nice warm cup of chamomile tea.

Weighted Blanket

A weighted blanket has been shown to relieve stress and anxiety for many people, including those who suffer from ADHD. Children who suffer from neuro developmental disorders often need deep pressure. Your son may also have an issue with proprioception, which means they also struggle to understand where their body is in relation to space.

The weighted blanket continuously puts pressure on their muscles and joints over the entire night. This helps calm their nervous system and regulate their inability to sense themselves.

Exercise

Exercise has a lot of really great benefits. One of the best benefits attached to exercising is that it will help wear your child out. If they are involved in organized sports, martial arts, or even go outside to play or ride their bike, it will help them expend all their extra energy. When it is time to come in and go to bed, they will be ready—at least physically. It increases the time that they spend in deep sleep, which is extremely important to getting a good night's rest. In addition, exercising during the day means their body will transition between sleep phases easier.

Won't. Stay. In. Bed.

This is what your sentences sound like after they've been out of bed several times. First, they refused to go to bed and it took an act of congress to finally get them between the sheets. Then, three minutes later, surprise —there they are again.

Children who suffer from ADHD, especially if they have oppositional defiance disorder or suffer from anxiety, tend to avoid bed at all costs. Once you are finally able to get them into bed, they act like a jack in the box and pop up every five seconds.

ADDitude magazine recommends a behavioral approach to handle this problem. You have to give your child strict and direct instructions that your child stays in bed between certain hours. Then, you would sit outside their door to make sure that they follow orders.

When they do get out of bed, you would calmly put them back. Then, in a gentle, albeit firm, voice, tell them it's time for sleep. Tell them that you will be very close if they need you. After a couple of nights, they will understand that popping out isn't going to work, and they will stay in bed and you can give up your post.

This technique is stressful, so you and your partner will have to stick with it until your child stays in bed. Abandoning your post for even one night will make the tactic not work.

. . .

If All Else Fails

When nothing else seems to work, talk to their doctor. It could be their medication combined with their ADHD, making it very difficult to sleep. Their medication could be adjusted so they can take it earlier in the day and it won't affect them at night. They might also be prescribed a medication that doesn't last as long, so the effects have worn off by bedtime.

Eating Right

A good diet is extremely important for all children, and even more so for children who suffer from ADHD. There are several nutritional elements that are extremely important for children. There are other dieting tips that are important for children with ADHD.

One tip is to make sure to eat balanced meals. Sometimes it can be very hard, especially at night, to make a full course meal. After all, you've worked all day, played chauffer to your children, made sure they got to all of their events on time, and now they are about to execute a mutiny because they are *starving to death*.

There are ways to make this a little less arduous.

- You can prepare meals ahead of time and freeze them, so they can just be heated up during the week.
- Get your kids to help you. Not only does this take some of the pressure off of you and teach your child valuable skills, but it also gives you and your children the opportunity to bond.
- There are companies you can subscribe to that deliver specific types of meal kits. Everything is pre-measured and ready for you to cook.
- Make your own meal kits. You can buy all the needed ingredients ahead of time and have them prepared (on the weekend perhaps), so all you have to do is throw everything together.

Just like everything else we've discussed, it is important that meal times and snacks are scheduled around the same time every day. Not only does this help with your child's mental state when they know what is happening and at what time, but it will also help them physically. Their body will become accustomed to eating dinner at six. It will also help them maintain a healthy blood sugar level.

Don't let them skip meals. If they skip a meal, especially if their body is accustomed to eating at a certain time, their blood sugar levels could crash. In addition, it could lead to the searching for unhealthy snacks.

Keep healthy snacks on hand. Fruits, nuts, and chopped vegetables are perfect snacks to help tame your son's rumbling belly until their next meal. They also have a lot of important vitamins and minerals to help decrease the symptoms of their ADHD.

Ask the doctor if they have any recommendations for multivitamins. This can be especially important if your child is a picky eater, and you couldn't get them to drink the strawberry, banana, and spinach smoothie.

Check the labels on any food that you buy for artificial preservatives, colors, and additives.

Check out the perimeter of the store, because this is generally where the grocers stash the least processed foods.

Exercise

Are you one of the people who gets up extra early in the morning to jog a couple miles or follow an exercise routine? If so, that is terrific. It is also a great way to help your child.

Some studies have shown that if your child exercises for about half an hour before school, it can help him control the symptoms of their ADHD and help them be in a better mood. Studies suggest that exercising before school can even decrease the amount of stimulant medications he needs to take to function well in school.

Exercise helps increase the brain's production of neurotransmitters, such as dopamine. In addition, exercise increases the amount of brain-derived neurotrophic factor (BDNF), which helps your brain make stronger connections. Increased levels of BDNF have a direct correlation to better learning rates.

ADDitude magazine explained, "Exercise primes the brain for learning, and environmental enrichment helps to make the important connections happen. When kids with ADHD are stimulated in class, following exercise, it encourages the newly developed cells to plug into the brain's communication network and become members of the signaling community."

The magazine recommends that your child run, skip, jump, or engage in other types of physical exercise for half an hour at least four times a week before they head off to school to exercise their brain. Exercising after school and before homework can be very important as well.

Although exercising is great, not all exercises are created equally. There are some exercise ideas that are especially helpful for your child to build their focus. ADDitude magazine recommends the following sports.

1. Swimming is a great sport for children who suffer from ADHD. Swimmers often receive individual attention from their coaches while benefiting from being a part of a team. They will be able to focus on their own personal development without having to compete with their teammates. Their goal is to improve their own swim times.

2. Martial arts is another sport that can help children with ADHD. First, martial arts have specific routines and rituals, such as bowing to the sensei. In addition, martial arts have a lot of structure. Students master the art by following step-by-step instructions. Not only does this help prevent the students from becoming distracted, but it also helps children who struggle to follow a complex set of instructions.

3. Tennis is another sport recommended for children with ADHD. This sport would help your child by encouraging them to compete with themselves and focus on constantly improving their game. They don't have to coordinate with team members. An added bonus is that it is a really great stress relief if they've had a frustrating day at school.

4. Gymnastics has been shown to help children with ADHD. The individual sport would help your child improve their focus because they have to pay close attention to the way their body moves. It can also help them improve their senses and help them develop their core strength, increase their awareness of their muscles, and improve their balance.

5. Wrestling might be a good sport for your child if they seem to have a lot of extra energy and perhaps a smidge of aggression. This sport would help them challenge those two elements, which would normally get them into trouble, into a positive way to avoid trouble. It is the only place where your child can knock someone down without getting detention, or worse.

6. Soccer is a great sport because it lets your child be a part of a

team. Play is constant, and your child could be running for a full 90 minutes, depending on their position.

7. Equine-assisted therapy was discussed in one of the earlier chapters. Making a connection with an animal, especially a horse, could have a number of incredible benefits for children with ADHD. Working with horses is calming and relaxing. Horses also give off great social cues, which could be important since many children with ADHD struggle to understand their peers' social cues.

8. As you know, running is a great way for your child to release pent up energy. That means they could be your track or cross country star. These sports are great because in order to succeed, your child has to learn to discipline and pace themselves. Like gymnastics, it can also teach them to pay attention to their body because runners assume a certain form to run faster and longer. In addition, track is a team sport where they can learn important social skills.

9. Although you might quiver at the thought of putting a bow and arrow in your child's hands, archery is another sport that can help your child. It teaches responsibility, first and foremost. In addition, it helps improve concentration while building their confidence.

10. Baseball is another potential sport to help your child, although you might need to work with their coach to keep your child from getting bored. The coach might give them a job to do between your child's turn on the field. They might also let your child learn new positions.

Talk to the Coach

Regardless of sport, it is just as important to talk to the coach as it is to work with your child's classroom teachers. Tell the coach about your child's ADHD and their particular symptoms. Let the coach know the best ways to handle discipline. Being forced to run suicides is more likely to make them angry than it is to help them learn to focus.

Ask the coach if they can talk with your child to make sure that they understand the instructions and rules. Also, tell the coach that it would help if your child can do a task during down time.

It is important to work with the coach in determining what strengths your child has and how to help your child grow.

One of the key things in helping your child be successful is to make sure they stick with it, even if they get frustrated and want to quit.

Hobbies

Hobbies are a great way to help your child learn to focus. Depending on the hobby, they might also help with learning how to follow step-by-step instructions. They can help your child explore a topic that they have shown a lot of interest and talent in. There are clubs that focus on a lot of hobbies, so joining a group of peers who have the same interests can be a huge help in getting him to learn great social skills.

Dinosaurs, civil war battles, rock collecting, and stamp collecting are all common interests for kids. They might enjoy writing music or playing an instrument. Drama groups and reading clubs are also great outlets for those who enjoy these types of activities. Building Lego structures, putting together puzzles, or building bridges with popsicle sticks might interest your child if they live logistics and math. Ask your child what interests them. They might need to try a few different hobbies until they find one that suits their interests and personalities.

Games

Games can be a great asset for children who suffer from ADHD. Some games, such as chess, checkers, Clue, and Monopoly would require that your child plans ahead. It means they have to pay attention for longer time periods. It also requires them to think before they act. These types of games stimulate metacognition and working memory.

Of course, almost all kids love video games. In cases where they can't sit for five minutes to read a book in class, they can sit in front of the television for hours at a time without moving anything but their fingers.

There are several problem solving games that can benefit your child, such as *The Legend of Zelda, Command & Conquer,* and *Sim City.* These games require that your child pay attention for longer periods. It also means they have to think about their actions before they make them. Another great benefit is that it means they have to set goals and figure out how to meet those goals.

One popular game, *Minecraft,* would help them plan their moves and improve their working memory. *Roblox* and *Bad Piggies* are other game choices with the same potential benefits.

Fantasy sports teams are other game choices that could help your child. These games require your child to manage their time and initiate tasks. They require a lot of executive functioning skills.

"Green Therapy"

Spending more time outdoors and in nature—referred to as green therapy—has been shown to have phenomenal benefits for kids who suffer from ADHD. Spending more time in nature helps improve your child's attention. Being outside among the trees, bushes, and grass often gives your child more room to burn off extra energy. In addition, studies have shown that just being outdoors, regardless of the activity, the setting itself seems to have a positive effect on hyperactivity.

In addition, being in parks and other types of green spaces has a direct effect on reducing aggression, mental fatigue, emotional fatigue, and other negative behaviors. Being in natural areas helps improve impulsivity and self-discipline. It also improves immunity and short term memory. Being in nature reduces stress and the body's production of stress hormones, such as cortisol. It increases the levels of vitamin D.

There are many studies that back up the idea that green therapy has a tremendous effect on children who suffer from ADHD. One study had children take a 20-minute walk in three different settings. One setting was a park. The other two settings were a neighborhood and an urban area. The urban area was a well-kept space. The noise levels in all three of the areas were similar. Prior to the test, the children were asked to solve a puzzle, which was designed to promote attentional fatigue for each. Then, after the walk, they were asked to perform a task. Not only did the children who walked in the park perform better, but the walk in the park seemed to help them as much as a dose of Ritalin would.

There are a lot of ways that you and your child can get more green time.

1. Walks and bike rides on nature paths.
2. Camping. The American Camp Association is a great resource for helping you to find the perfect summer camp for your child.
3. Check out your local recreation center for activities and field trips that involve the outdoors.
4. Let your child plan a picnic in the backyard or at the park.

5. Encourage your child to practice their hobby outside, such as reading or making craft projects.
6. If possible, encourage them to get involved in a pick up basketball game.
7. Gardening is a great outdoor hobby that has a lot of terrific benefits.
8. You can set up a scavenger hunt for your child. If they are older, you can create clues that show them where the objects are. It might be fun if they set one up for you, as well.
9. Go hiking with your child at a state park.
10. Grab a book on nature that features local birds, wildlife, and plants. Then, have an expedition where you and your child try to find examples of these.

The possibilities are endless.

AFTERWORD

Good health is very important for everyone. It is extremely important that children who suffer from ADHD are healthy because physical health has a direct connection to mental health. In this case, the healthier your child is, the more manageable their ADHD symptoms will be.

Although it is sometimes difficult to make your child understand that sleep is extremely important to helping them manage their ADHD symptoms, sleep is essential. Depending on your child's age, they will need at least eight to ten hours of sleep each night. If your child struggles to sleep, then there are several remedies that you can try. Once a ritual is established, the bedtime process will be a lot easier.

As discussed earlier, diet is extremely important in many ways. Proteins, omega-3 fatty acids, and complex carbohydrates are important for children who suffer from ADHD. Keeping meal and snack times on a routine and making sure you stock healthy snacks can make a huge difference for your child.

Multiple studies have shown that exercise and green time have a tremendously positive effect on children who suffer from ADHD. They can help increase dopamine, which is the neurotransmitter that children with ADHD often lack. They also help their attention span and the development of social skills. It can calm your child and get them to follow step-by-step instructions.

Potentially, healthy activities could reduce your child's ADHD symptoms and their need for medication.

Chapter Summary

- The link between a healthy body and mind is undeniable.
- Getting plenty of sleep and exercise are important for good health.
- Green therapy has been shown to improve symptoms for children who suffer from ADHD.

In the next chapter, you will learn about other mental health issues your child might face and how to help them.

CHAPTER NINE: OTHER MENTAL HEALTH ISSUES THAT ACCOMPANY ADHD

*A*s if you and your child didn't have enough to deal with, there are other mental health issues that children with ADHD might face. According to MentalHelp.net, approximately 60 to 80 percent of all children who suffer from ADHD will also struggle with another mental health disorder.

The good news is that many of these problems are treated with the same type of therapies and techniques used to help decrease the intensity of the symptoms of ADHD.

This chapter talks about the more common of these mental health issues, how they present themselves, and potential ways to treat them.

Oppositional Defiant Disorder

Oppositional defiant disorder (ODD) may be an issue for 20 to 60 percent of children who suffer from ADHD. The symptoms are more obvious with people the child is close to, such as family members, teachers, and other caregivers.

One symptom is that they might argue with adults when asked to do something or obey a rule. They might also flat out refuse to obey the rules. They may often become angry, resentful, or even show signs of being vindictive. They might go out of their way to annoy other people, and they could also become easily annoyed with others. They might refuse to take responsibility for their actions and mistakes, choosing instead to put the blame on others.

There are different levels of ODD. If your child suffers from a mild version, they would only display their symptoms in one setting, such as at school, home, or in social settings. Moderate is when their symptoms show up in two settings. Severe ODD is when their symptoms occur in three or more settings. Sometimes, their symptoms will be displayed in one setting and eventually grow to more.

Oppositional defiant disorder can cause a lot of other issues to manifest. They might demonstrate poor performance at school. They might also display a lot of antisocial behaviors. They might not be able to control their impulsiveness. More severe issues, such as substance abuse problems and suicidal tendencies may become a problem.

Opposing authority might be an indication that your child is developing, or already has, ODD. However, it might also be because your child is struggling to interact with what is going on around them. If you see symptoms start to occur, then you should seek treatment as soon as possible. If it is a precursor to ODD, then early treatment may stop ODD from developing fully.

Treatments generally comprise family-based therapy. In addition, your child might receive psychotherapy and behavioral therapy. Although medications might be prescribed for ODD, they will not be the only form of treatment.

Parenting training is one form of therapy that can be used to help your child. The therapist will help you develop more positive parenting techniques. Sometimes, your child will also be involved in this training so you, your child, and your therapist can work together to develop goals and determine how to achieve those goals.

Individual therapy for your child can help them learn how to manage their anger and frustration better and find more constructive ways to communicate their feelings with people.

Family therapy can help your family learn how to work together, improve communication, and improve your overall relationship as a familial unit.

Cognitive problem solving training will help your child identify thought patterns that cause their behavioral issues, and then learn how to change those thought patterns.

Collaborative problem solving is a therapy technique designed to help you and your child work together to develop solutions to your problems.

Social skills training is another therapy technique that can be used to help treat ODD.

To help your child, you can give them specific, clear instructions that they need to follow. When they don't, you need to follow through with the appropriate consequences. Praising your child when they do well is also very important.

It is crucial that you remind your child that they are loved and accepted, even if they have some issues that you, as a family, need to work on.

Also remember to be kind to yourself. Having a child with ADHD and ODD is extremely hard and would test the patience of a saint.

Depression

Depression is more than just feeling sad; it is a mental illness that can cause extreme behavioral changes. Between ten and 30 percent of children with ADHD also suffer from depression. Children may demonstrate their depression differently than adults. Their hyperactivity and impulsive behavior may increase. They might also become more irritable. Other symptoms might be if your child is in a *low* mood, if they are no longer interested in their favorite activities, or pulls away from their friends. Changes in their eating and sleeping patterns may also be an indication of depression. Neglecting schoolwork and homework, and falling grades can be other indications. Being more spacey and acting out more are also signs of depression. If they take about feeling hopeless about their life, or helpless about what is going on around them, and especially if they talk about suicide, you have to get help immediately.

There are a couple of causes of depression. One is environmental. Your child might develop depression if they view their environment as unpredictable, as ADHD children need to have an organized and structured life. Another cause is if they perceive their peers to be mean to them, or if they reject them. Depression might also appear if your child perceives school to be overwhelming and negative.

MentalHelp.net stated that if their depression is caused by environmental reasons, then specific treatment for their depression might be unnecessary because their environment will improve as their ADHD improves.

On the other hand, depression can be hereditary. If this is the case, then a separate treatment plan might be necessary.

To determine which could be the cause, you have to determine which came first—the ADHD or the depression.

Regardless of what caused the depression, it is important to take the symptoms very seriously. Depression, especially when accompanied by ADHD, can cause your child to have suicidal thoughts or tendencies.

If your child is diagnosed with depression, the doctor can prescribe them antidepressants to help stabilize their mood. It is important that the psychiatrist or medical doctor who prescribes the antidepressants understands that your child is also taking medications for their ADHD, so the two medications don't interfere with each other and cause even more harm. It is important to talk about potential side effects of the medications with your doctor and pharmacist.

Therapy is also beneficial. One type of therapy that might help your child cope with depression is cognitive behavioral therapy, discussed in chapter two.

Dialectical behavior therapy (DBT) is a form of CBT that was created to help people with more severe depression, such as those who are more prone to suicide or hurting themselves in other ways, such as cutting. This type of therapy uses mindfulness, which is about being fully present in the moment, focusing on only one thing, and not judging. It also helps your child develop their problem solving skills and learn how to deal with stressful situations. This therapy also helps your child learn social skills so they can have better interactions with friends and family.

Another therapy technique for depression is interpersonal psychotherapy (IPT). Because social relationships often suffer when your child is having a depressive episode, IPT helps your child's relationships become healthier. Your child will learn how to communicate their thoughts and feelings better, so friends and family know how to be supportive. In addition, they will learn how to solve conflicts. An important aspect of this therapy is that they will be able to tell when a relationship is influencing how they feel.

Mindfulness based cognitive therapy (MBCT) combines CBT with mindfulness. Both of these techniques were discussed in earlier chapters.

Neurofeedback therapy has been shown to help people who suffer from depression by teaching them how to alter their brainwaves.

Many therapists believe that the families should be involved in the therapy sessions as well. Therapists can help you understand how to deal with your child's depression and help them. It is important for you to understand that your child might try to isolate themselves from everyone.

They might also perceive even the most positive words and actions as negative. A therapist can help you learn when you need to back away from your child and give them some space, and when it is time to get closer and offer your support.

It is also very important that you understand the skills and techniques your child is using to help them cope with their depression, so you can help them use them.

Dealing with a child who is suffering from ADHD is hard enough, but when depression comes calling, it makes your job even harder—mentally, emotionally, and physically. It is extremely important that you take care of yourself in all ways. If you need to, seek therapy for yourself. Sometimes, it just helps to talk to an unbiased observer.

Anxiety

Anxiety is more than simple nervousness. The Mayo Clinic defines it as a disorder in which you "... frequently have intense, excessive, and persistent worry and fear about everyday situations. Often, anxiety disorders involve repeated episodes of sudden feelings of intense anxiety and fear or terror that reach a peak within minutes (panic attacks)."

Approximately one quarter of people who suffer from ADHD also suffer from an anxiety disorder.

There are several symptoms that you should watch for. Low self-esteem, unpredictable mood swings, fatigue, excessive grumpiness, an unwillingness to try anything new, feeling as though they are unable to accomplish any tasks, physical pain, and missing a lot of school. They may display learned helplessness, which means they believe it doesn't really matter what they do, it won't make a difference in their life.

The stimulant medication their doctor prescribes for their ADHD may actually cause symptoms of an anxiety disorder to worsen. If you believe your child might have an anxiety disorder, you should talk to their doctor because they may be feeling anxious without having an anxiety disorder. This means the treatments would be different.

Anxiety disorders can disrupt life in a lot of ways. It might cause your child to suffer from depression. It could also lead to substance abuse problems, insomnia, headaches, and digestive problems. It could cause social withdrawal or even suicide.

There are different types of anxiety disorders. Generalized anxiety disorder (GAD) is present if your child worries every day about everything. It is more than just worrying over a test or regular things that most people worry about. They might worry about war, the future, recess, lunch time, death, or just about anything else you may not even think about. This type of anxiety makes it difficult for your child to have fun, eat well, or even go to sleep. Some children with this disorder talk about it with other people, but others don't. If they do share their worries with you, no amount of comforting can ease their mind.

Separation anxiety disorder (SAD) is another type. It is normal for babies and younger children to experience separation anxiety. However, for some children, it continues even as they get older. They will refuse to go to school, on playdates, or any other activity that would require them to be separated from their family. They might even have trouble falling asleep in their own room.

Social anxiety disorder, or social phobia, causes children to be extremely afraid of what other people will think of them. They might be afraid that others believe they are strange or weird. They don't like it when other people notice them, don't participate in class, and do not like working in groups.

Some children suffer from a form of selective mutism. This is when a child's anxiety is so intense that they don't talk. They are able to speak, they just refuse to do so in schools, with peers, or in other places.

Specific phobias are another form of anxiety disorder. A common one for children is being afraid of the dark. Many children have an extreme fear of loud noises, clowns, dogs, etc. If your child has this type of anxiety disorder, they would go out of their way to avoid any place that would put them in contact with the object of their fear.

Similar to depression, many therapy options for anxiety are the same ones that might be treating their ADHD. Cognitive behavioral therapy is one option for your child. Behavior therapy is yet another. Art therapy may also help your child.

Exercise, eating healthy, and getting enough sleep are also important to help reduce symptoms of anxiety disorders. Meditation, mindfulness, yoga, and breathing exercises are other methods that can be used.

Deep pressure therapy may also help your child. Weighted blankets, weighted vests, and similar items may help. One of my clients carries around a special weighted sloth as he goes through the school day, and it has helped him immeasurably.

A stress ball or other similar object may also help. Not only does the squeezing motion itself help, but it can also give them something else to think about besides what is causing them anxiety.

You can help your child as well. Praise them when they face their fears. Help them practice ways to cope if they encounter their fears. Listen to them when they talk and don't dismiss their fears. Avoid saying things like, "Don't be silly. There's nothing in the dark that isn't in the light."

Bipolar Disorder

Approximately half of boys and a quarter of the girls who suffer from bipolar disorder also suffer from ADHD.

One sign of bipolar disorder is frequent mood swings. They might be hyperactive, aggressive, impulsive, or socially inappropriate. They might also engage in risky behavior, such as drinking or other substance abuse. They might not be able to sleep, have depressive episodes, be grumpy, or even suicidal. They might also have inflated views of themselves and their capabilities. They may have rags or explosive temper tantrums that go on for hours. They may not be able to focus on homework or other tasks. They may be uncharacteristically giddy or silly or have more energy than they normally do. Their mind might race, or they might display rapid speech.

It is important that your doctor does a thorough physical of your child, as the symptoms of ADHD and bipolar disorder are very similar.

Bipolar disorder can be treated with medication. It is extremely important that the doctor and pharmacist are aware of all medications that your child is taking because it is important that they be given medication that doesn't interact with their ADHD medication.

Talk therapy may also help your child. Cognitive behavior therapy, behavior therapy, art therapy, and similar types of therapy may help your child. Often, the family is involved in these types of therapy. When one member of the family suffers from mental health issues, it often affects everyone in the family. It is also beneficial if the whole family understands how they can help your child deal with their bipolar disorder.

In addition, neurofeedback therapy has been shown to help some people who suffer from bipolar disorder or depression.

If your child begins to engage in extremely risky behavior or self-harm, such as cutting themselves, or talks about suicide, their doctor might recommend a stay at a psychiatric hospital or a treatment center.

It is important that you work in close contact with your child's school. If their symptoms interfere with their or their classmates' education, then a behavior plan might be beneficial. A modified schedule may help them, as could a special pass that would allow them to visit the counselor or social worker at school whenever they need.

Meditation, yoga, and mindfulness may be beneficial to your child. Don't forget the "green therapy," as it could also be beneficial.

Talk to your child and listen to their feelings. It is important to validate their thoughts and feelings, as they are very real. You can help your child develop plans to cope with potentially stressful situations.

Sensory Integration Disorder

Sensory integration disorder can either be mistaken for ADHD or coexist with ADHD.

Carol Kranowitz, a special education teacher and expert on ADHD and sensory disorders, stated that in addition to the traditional five senses that we learn at a young age (taste, smell, touch, hearing, and sight) there are three additional senses that most people are unaware of. The vestibule sense is the master sense. This sense helps people know where they are, whether they are moving, and if so, how fast they are moving, whether they're falling, etc.

The proprioception sense is the sense related to muscles and joints. This helps people know how to move, such as walking up stairs or getting dressed.

The interoception sense is the sense related to the internal organs. These senses tell you when it's time to eat or take care of other important body functions.

When the senses are working properly, they keep you safe and provide you with satisfaction. Nothing is better than smelling that tamale right before you taste it. Nothing beats hearing your child tell you they love you right before they put your arms around your neck for a hug. The senses also help you execute the actions that your brain has planned out.

Sometimes, though, the senses get out of whack. The senses might respond to certain stimuli late, never, or inappropriately. There are three main types of sensory disorder, and each type has a subtype associated with it.

Sensory Modulation

Sensory modulation is how the brain manages the amount of sensory input it pays attention to at any given time. When the brain's sensory modulation is working correctly, your brain will filter out any information that is irrelevant, so that it can deal with the important information. Children can suffer from one or all of the different subtypes. The symptoms might be mistaken for ADHD, or they could coexist with ADHD.

People who suffer from sensory over responsiveness tend to have an elevated sensitivity to information. It is as though they are constantly being barraged with information. According to Pediatric Therapy and Learning Center, "As a result, these individuals often experience a 'fight, flight, or fright' response to these sensations which their bodies feel either too easily, too quickly, or too intensely." Signs of this is if your child tends to cover their ears in order to avoid loud sounds or being touched. Other signs may be an inability to focus, aggressiveness, or hyperactivity.

Individuals who suffer from sensory under responsiveness do not respond to information well. They might act passive because they are not able to respond to the information their senses provide. They might seem clumsy, or use too little or too much force when doing things, such as opening a door, because they are not responding to touch and pressure. They may also be unable to notice temperature changes or feel pain as much. Signs of this issue could be inattention, decreased interest level, decreased activity levels, daydreaming a lot, and craving opportunities to move around a lot.

Sensory seeking/craving is the third subtype. People who suffer from this subtype are very active and never seem to become tired in their pursuit of sensory information. They are the children who have to touch everything (including the red button), and they may not respect people's personal bubbles. Signs of this include hyperactivity, impulsiveness, the need to be stimulated constantly, risk taking, and being easily excitable.

Sensory Discrimination

Sensory discrimination is the ability to tell the difference between the different types of sensory input that you are receiving and the sensations.

There are different subtypes of this sensory issue. One type is auditory discrimination, where your child might have a problem determining where and from whom sounds are coming from. They might also have difficulties determining the difference between words that sound the same.

People who suffer from visual discrimination might have a hard time telling the difference between people's faces and finishing puzzles, and they can *never* succeed at the game, *Where's Waldo.*

Tactile discrimination is when your child has problems determining the difference between the way things feel. Olfactory discrimination affects the ability to determine the difference between smells, whereas gustatory discrimination affects determining the difference between tastes.

Vestibular discrimination issues result in your child having problems with balance, hand-eye coordination, and movement. It can make it difficult for your child to determine the direction and speed of their movement and even learn the difference between right and left.

Proprioceptive discrimination problems may be mistaken for clumsiness. When this is present, your child may have problems determining where their body is in space. It can make grading of force difficult, which is how hard they push open a door or pet the family cat. It can make it difficult for them to use a pencil or walk up a staircase without consciously watching their feet.

Sensory Based Motor Disorder

Sensory based motor disorder is when your child has problems with balance, fine motor skills, large motor skills, and the ability to perform motor actions, whether these actions are familiar or new.

Postural disorder may cause your child to struggle with their movements. Their movements might be clumsy, and they may trip themselves. Dyspraxia is the inability to come up with new ideas for items they are familiar with. They might be able to use a piece of paper for writing or drawing, but they might not be able to come up with the idea of making a paper airplane.

How You Can Help

Getting your child outside and playing is the best way to help them. Playing outside lets your child use their senses. Because the brain can change and grow, the best way to help them bolster their senses is to let them use them.

Touch is one way to help your child. Hug them when they are having a problem. Teach them to squeeze their arm or leg if they are stressed.

Occupational therapy is often used to treat sensory disorders.

Of course, if you think your child has a sensory disorder, it is important to talk to their doctor to find the right treatment.

Learning Disorder

Approximately 30 to 50 percent of all children who suffer from ADHD also have a learning disability. A learning disability affects how your child learns. Learning disabilities do not have anything to do with intelligence or how hard your child is trying; it is simply that they process information differently.

There are several learning disorders that may accompany ADHD, such as dyslexia, dysgraphia, dyspraxia, and dyscalculia (problems with reading, writing, motor skills, and math, respectively).

Learning disabilities can cause your child to have low self-esteem. They can cause behavior problems, especially as they try to avoid tasks that they normally struggle with. They might also feel isolated from their peers.

There are a lot of ways you can help your child.

First, if you suspect they have a learning disability, contact their school. The school is obligated under the IDEA to evaluate your child.

If they do have a learning disability, then you can work with the school to create an IEP plan for them, which will not only create goals for progress, but it will also develop specific methods to help them succeed. This might include special tutoring, technology, or other tools.

Substance Abuse

Many people who suffer from ADHD develop substance abuse problems, most commonly alcohol and marijuana, which usually leads to the abuse of cocaine. However, Mental.Help.net stated that the connection between ADHD and substance abuse is decreased when the individual is on medication to help regulate their symptoms.

AFTERWORD

The symptoms caused by ADHD are hard enough to deal with. However, ADHD is often accompanied by other mental health issues that can make life even more difficult. With medication, therapy, and other treatment methods, and of course, your loving support, your child will be successful in life.

It is exceedingly important to take care of yourself. This cannot be stressed enough. If you aren't taking care of yourself physically, mentally, and emotionally, you won't be able to help your child as much as you want to. Partake in some of that "green therapy" yourself. Make sure you are exercising and eating right, as well as getting enough sleep. When you get stressed, try out one of the meditation techniques, a new yoga pose, or just breathe.

Chapter Summary

- ADHD is often accompanied by other mental health issues.
- It is important to be able to determine the difference between the symptoms of mental health issues and ADHD.
- Although additional health problems can make life a little more difficult, they are all still treatable, and with your love and support, your child can still come out with a successful life.

EXCERPTS FROM MY NEXT BOOK: ANGER MANAGEMENT TIPS FOR PARENTS

*R*aising children takes a lot of patience. They don't come with how-to manuals, and the ones that do exist are not of the one-size-fits-all variety. Every child is different and has a different personality. They can be amazing. They are sweet, loveable, and so much fun. They make life so much more enjoyable.

And sometimes, they are defiant, cranky, and go out of their way to get on your very last nerve, as though it was an Olympic event.

There are a lot of times when you can feel the steam start to come out of your ears and you are going to explode.

It is very important that you take a step back and breathe. Send your child to their room so they can think about their actions while you calm down.

There are many reasons why controlling your temper is extremely important.

Importance of Anger Management
Teaches a valuable lesson
Your child is no fool. They know exactly what they did, that it was wrong, and you are angry.

If you take a step away from the situation until you can calm down and think clearly, then they will learn that is the best way to handle anger.

On the other hand, if you lash out, then you are teaching them that lashing out is the best way to handle a situation.

Anger equals regrettable actions and words

When you are angry, you aren't using your logic and reason. Anger causes the flight or fight response to kick in. This means that the majority of your blood and oxygen are going to your muscles, so you have the strength to fight whatever battle is in front of you with very little going to your brain. This is why getting angry is called getting mad. Mad is another way of saying insanity.

During this period of brief insanity, you may say things that you wouldn't ordinarily say to your child. Unfortunately, you can't take back your words, and no amount of apologies later can ever erase hurtful words from your child's head.

You may also do things you wouldn't normally do. Spankings can become beatings. A quick pop to the mouth for a smart comment might be delivered with a lot more force than you meant for it to.

It is better to wait until you can choose your words and actions carefully.

Health issues

Anger and frustration cause a wide range of health issues, especially if you are angry quite frequently. Some children are good at pushing those buttons over and over again.

Anger causes heart disease, high blood pressure, insomnia, and other problems. It is extremely important that you can control your anger and frustration.

Family problems

A lot of anger can cause family problems. It is hard to maintain a relationship with someone who is angry often. It causes tension in the home. In addition, anger issues cause aggression and can lead to violence.

When You Become Angry

There are several ways to handle your anger when your adorable cherub once again upset you.

Calm down

Controlling your breathing is a great way to help calm your anger. It allows you to focus on something besides your annoyance and frustration. Breathing also directly affects your muscles, brain, and other parts of your body, helping you achieve calmness.

Picturing a place, object, animal, or something else in your mind can help as well. It helps you focus on an image instead of the situation.

Have a specific word or phrase that you can repeat to yourself. If you are religious, you might repeat a psalm or something similar. If not, then you can sing a specific song, or even just say, "tree, tree, tree."

Resolving the issue

Listen to your child. Make sure you understand clearly what your child is trying to say. Repeat what they are saying back to them. Then, calmly explain your perspective, and then have them repeat it back to you. Then, you can take appropriate actions. "I understand that you were hungry, but eating the cookies before dinner was not acceptable, especially since I told you not to. Therefore, you are grounded from your phone for..."

Think logically. Most of the time, your child isn't really trying to make you angry; they just didn't think about the consequences of their actions before they did them.

Remember that they are human, and humans make mistakes.

Avoid generalizing. Don't tell him that they "never clean their room" or they "never listen."

Remember to praise them when they do well.

Know yourself and when you are about to blow up. Count to ten before you say or do something you might regret. Leave the room for a minute.

Use "I" instead of "you." Tell them "I am frustrated when you don't listen" instead of "you frustrate me when you don't listen." It will keep them from becoming defensive and shutting down. After all, your goal in raising your child is to teach them right from wrong. If they shut down, they can't learn the lesson.

The same goes for the flip side. Your child may try to criticize or upset you. Don't get defensive because then it will be harder to resolve the situation. Don't attack back. "I'm sorry you feel that way, but the fact is, you ate the cookies and I told you not to."

Humor can sometimes diffuse the situation, but don't make fun of your child. That will only escalate the situation.

Take a break before you handle a situation. If you're already stressed or just had a long, hard day at work, don't deal with the situation immediately. Take a ten or 15 minute break to relax.

Long-Term Methods for Anger Management

Sometimes, anger comes from everyday frustrations or stress. You got to work five minutes late, the line at the gas station was long, someone put mustard on your sandwich instead of mayo, your boss was cranky, and your child ate an entire bag of cookies right before dinner.

It wasn't so much that they ate the cookies or disobeyed you that made you furious. It is all of the accumulated stressors and annoyances that have built up throughout the day. The cookies were simply the proverbial straw that broke the camel's back.

There are several ways you can reduce your stress. Not only will it make it easier to deal with your child when they choose to be a turkey, but it will also help you handle all the stressors thrown your way, and it will help you be healthier.

Meditation

Meditation is a great way to help you relax. There are many different meditation methods that you can engage in. It doesn't take very long, so you can meditate for five minutes or an hour.

You can also meditate anywhere. You can meditate at work, in your car, or even in the bathtub when you've locked yourself in the bathroom to get that five minutes of peace.

Yoga

Yoga is another way for you to relax. You would focus on your body and breathing and let your stresses slip your mind, at least for a while.

· · ·

Exercise

Not only is exercise a great way to be physically healthier, but it is also great for you to become emotionally healthier. Exercise increases your brain's production of dopamine, which is one of the chemicals that helps you feel happy and satisfied. It is very calming and can help reduce the stress you encounter throughout your day. It will make it a lot easier to handle those stressful situations with your children, as well.

Breathing Exercises

There are a number of breathing exercises that can help you manage your stress and anger. The purpose of breathing exercises is to have you breathe deeply and focus on your breathing. Breathing exercises have been proven to calm people physically and mentally.

Mindfulness

Mindfulness is about focusing on the moment. You might concentrate on a candle flame. When stray thoughts come in, acknowledge them without judgment, and then return your attention back to the flame. Mindfulness has also been proven to help calm a person's mind and body.

Counseling

Life can be overwhelming. Work, kids, bills, and everything else that is going on in the world can be incredible sources of stress. If you find that you are angry a lot, you might consider counseling. There is no shame in getting counseling. There are many different types of counseling services that you can engage in to help yourself and ensure that your relationship with your children is healthy.

My book, *Anger Management for Parents,* is a resource that can help you strengthen your relationship with your child and learn ways to understand your child. There are also a lot of tips to help you manage the stress and anger in your life. In addition, my book helps you understand your child if they suffer from common disabilities, such as autism and ADHD.

Although it may feel as if you are trying to swim uphill with your child, you are not alone. And one day, when your child is a successful, happy adult, you can sit back with a huge smile and say, "We did this."

∾

Sign up and get your **FREE** copy, with a simple photo on the <u>QR code</u>, hoping to help you have the healthy and fulfilling life you deserve!

With Love, *THERESA MILLER*

ACKNOWLEDGMENTS

Love this book? Don't forget to leave a review!

Every review matters, and it matters a *lot*.

Head over to Amazon/Audible, or wherever you purchased this book, to leave an *honest review* for me.

I thank you endlessly.

Made in the USA
Columbia, SC
31 August 2021